at Home in the Garden

at Home in the Garden

Creating Stylish Outdoor Rooms

Becke Davis

FRIEDMAN/FAIRFAX

PUBLISHERS

A FRIEDMAN/FAIRFAX BOOK

Please visit our website: www.metrobooks.com

© 2001 by Michael Friedman Publishing Group, Inc.

Library of Congress Cataloging-in-Publication Data available upon request.

ISBN 1-56799-733-3

Editor: Susan Lauzau
Art Director: Jeff Batzli
Designer: Jennifer Markson
Photography Editor: Kathleen Wolfe
Production Manager: Richela Morgan

Color separations by Leefung-Asco Printers Ltd.
Printed in U.S.A.

1 3 5 7 9 10 8 6 4 2

Distributed by Sterling Publishing Company, Inc.
387 Park Avenue South
New York, NY 10016
Distributed in Canada by Sterling Publishing
Canadian Manda Group
One Atlantic Avenue, Suite 105
Toronto, Ontario, Canada M6K 3E7
Distributed in Australia by
Capricorn Link (Australia) Pty Ltd.
P.O. Box 6651
Baulkham Hills, Business Centre, NSW 2153, Australia

DEDICATION

This book is dedicated to my family and friends,
with thanks for their constant support:

To my husband Marty—still amazed after all these years,

To my kids, Jessica (Howie D. 4-Ever!) and Jonathan (Laser Tag Rules!),

To "the cousins," Amy, Sarah, and Christie Leonard, Ivan and Emily Suttman Villars,

To Mom, the collector, and Dad, the golfer,

To my sisters, Connie Soper and Laura Leonard,

To my brothers, Thom and Russ Villars, and the rest of the family: Chris Suttman Villars, Dave Soper, Emily,
Louise and Jacques Zander, Dave, Carol and Hunter Adams, Jim and Toby Adams, Pat and Frank
Buckmaster, Derek and Vicki Carden, Dotty and Rocky Bridges, Gillian, Richard and Ben Joyner, Len and
Ivy Davis, Chris and Lisa Davis, Em and Pat Davis, Bertie and Iris Davis, Barry and Gina Davis, Alice
Davis, Olive Carden, Esther Dickinson, the thousands of other Davis relations, and "almost family"
Isabell Petersen

To our kids-by-friendship: Brittany Duncan, Jennifer Oprean, Elisabeth Thorpe, Lea Dell, and Dean and
Colin Miller,

To "old" friends Terrie Sartain, Pat Seiler, Kerry Erickson, Bunny Texidor, Gail Omclusik Landau, Eileen Lang,
Sue Hansen, Phil Woods, Sue Dunn, Cathy Foss, Patricia Lee, Jean Thorpe, and Valerie Williams

To "new" friends Kim Parnes, Donna Wooton, Kip Iannelli, Debby Reece, Diane Heinbokel, Eileen Murphy,
Susan Schenk, Donna Wooton, Alice Miller, Jean Wirthlin, and Rosanne Barg

To Joyce Ashley and Jeff Tindall for their invaluable help,

To my editor, Susan Lauzau, for keeping me busy and on my toes, to Helen Johnson for her cheerful
encouragement, to Rick Reuland for making me keep writing when I was feeling discouraged,
to the Literacy Council of West Clermont Local School District in Cincinnati,

And to everyone who wishes to "see a World in a grain of sand, and a Heaven in a wild flower."

William Blake, *Auguries of Innocence*

CONTENTS

INTRODUCTION

The famed nineteenth-century poet William Wordsworth once lamented that "the world is too much with us." He would be appalled at what the intervening decades have brought in the way of worldly intrusions: snarled traffic, shock jocks, frenetic workdays, and screaming headlines all make Wordsworth's words even more compelling today. With stress levels running high and privacy at an all-time low, many people have turned to nature—particularly their own gardens—as a way to restore their weary spirits.

While home is indeed a haven, it can be hard to avoid the intrusions of reality: telephone and television, laundry and dishes. The garden offers a retreat from these competing stresses. We can breathe in the fragrant air and relish the soothing sounds of grasses rustling in the breeze and birds chirping to their mates. Even garden "chores"—digging in the soil, carting mulch, snipping off passed flowers—are some how comforting. These simple, physical tasks connect us to the earth in a way that is reassuring. The fact that we can perform them outdoors in the warm sunshine, often in blissful solitude, only adds to gardening's charms.

But to feel at home in the garden, we must create gardens that feel more like homes. Many modern landscapes have unfortunately been designed to impress passersby rather than to provide a comfortable retreat for family and guests. Look down from an airplane sometime and notice how many houses seem to have been dropped into the center of a green sea of grass. The same houses, up close, are ringed by a tight turtle-neck of foundation plants, occasionally splashed with beds of brightly colored flowers or shaded by an awning of closely planted trees. This type of arrangement has dominated the suburban landscape in the latter half of the twentieth century; once air conditioning and television became the norm, people moved from the front porch into the living room to enjoy the conveniences of modern life, relegating "the yard" to a place to be passed through on the way into the house or observed through a window. As we enter a new century, we've begun to see gardening as a way to reclaim the outdoors.

In recent years, there has been a surge of interest in reviving older gardening traditions or devising new ones in which the house and landscape work together as an

OPPOSITE: *The terra-cotta face of the "green man"—half human, half plant—is a potent reminder of our close connection to nature. This ancient pagan figure, which symbolizes rebirth and the male ability to nurture the earth, has proven a popular accent for garden rooms. Here, the mysterious face, which is fitted as a fountain, is enshrined in a shadowy dell of hostas, ferns, and fecund foliage. The weathered terra-cotta pot is a perfect foil for the silvery leaves of lamium and the pale, bell-like flowers of the hosta.*

9

integrated whole. Instead of living separated from nature, we've begun to think of the garden as a crucial part of the home, and we've come to view both the house and the garden's hardscape elements—walls, paths, pergolas, and so on—as a part of the larger landscape.

Considering the garden as an additional room and giving it the same care and attention you'd devote to your living room or bedroom allows you to create a pleasing outdoor space where you and your family will want to spend time. A well-planned garden room can extend your living area into the outdoors, providing extra space for

RIGHT: *A porch or breezeway can serve as the perfect transition between interior and exterior rooms. This charming colonnaded space, with its vine-covered arches and sweetly set table, is part garden, part breakfast nook. Beyond, various areas of the garden are defined by low-growing evergreen hedges.*

11

entertainment or recreation. You might even wish to plan several garden rooms with different themes or purposes. Thinking of your yard as a series of rooms, each with its own special character but all linked by common elements, can establish a sense of connectedness both among the different garden rooms and between landscape and house. This approach also allows you to integrate wasted space at the side of the house (or any area that might otherwise be overlooked) into your garden plan.

And don't think that you need property befitting an English manor house to accomplish your dreams—the tiniest city lot can hide a secret garden, while a house sited in a suburban development can gain character with a beautifully designed garden room. Where acreage abounds, there are exciting possibilities for creating garden rooms within charming enclosures and that take advantage of sweeping vistas.

These outdoor rooms should be as personal as your living room, designed and decorated to reflect your own unique tastes and priorities. So sit back, relax, and open your mind to the possibilities of your new outdoor "addition."

Chapter One

BRINGING YOUR HOME INTO THE GARDEN

GARDEN ROOMS

PAGES 12-13: *At first glance, the loose stone floor of the seating area would seem to indicate a casual setting for this outdoor room, but a closer look reveals a framework that is quite formal, with some medieval design elements. A modern interpretation of the classical knot garden is worked here with tightly trimmed boxwood and silvery artemisia. At the center of the knot garden, an armillary sphere—an old astronomical instrument—with an elegant verdigris finish echoes the deep greens of the table, chairs, railing, and latticework. Trees, vines, and a stone wall separate this distinctive room from the rest of the world.*

OPPOSITE: *A dark, heavy gate partly hidden within a bower of rampant greenery conveys the very essence of a secret garden. Note that this is not the wild disarray of an overgrown, forgotten nook, but rather the careful design of a thriving garden. Silver-tinged leaves of a variegated ivy accent the delicate gold of nearby shrubs, while large glossy leaves, feathery ferns, and creeping plants rising between the stone steps all add to the forested feel of this wonderfully secluded entrance.*

14

We are a civilized people searching for our uncivilized past. Cooped up in buildings all day, we look for ways to connect with nature, ways that were unnecessary for our early ancestors, who lived in close harmony with the natural world. Today we strive to reestablish this link with nature in part by bringing the outdoors in—by incorporating into our homes and offices large windows, skylights, miniature greenhouses, and even atriums or solariums that will let in the sun. We fill our interiors with hanging baskets, towering tropicals, potted herbs, and houseplants of all shapes and sizes. We dry flowers, cut flowers, even force flowers to bloom from branches brought indoors before the ground has thawed. From the time the very first flower was plucked and put into a clay jar, humans have been inviting the beauty of nature into their homes.

The concept of sending the indoors sprawling outward—extending the usable space of the house into the exterior landscape—is not new either. In ancient times houses wrapped around gardens, creating lovely open-air courtyards. The Persians developed their courtyards into lavish "paradise" gardens, while the Romans often used theirs as reception halls or living rooms. Terraced gardens extended from the stately manors of Britain or were carved into Italian hillsides during the Renaissance period, while vegetables and herbs were contained in accessible, though rarely prominent, plots at the back of the estate. Landscapes of this era—and to some extent, those of medieval times—were often divided into theme gardens: cutting gardens, formal rose beds, edged herb gardens, medicinal gardens, naturalized woodland areas, ornamental water gardens, and even bizarre topiary gardens. These theme gardens were often edged with walls or hedges that clearly outlined the boundaries between each type of garden.

In the early 1900s, American Lawrence Johnston purchased Hidcote Manor in England's Cotswolds and created a landscape masterpiece. He used hedges to define a

BRINGING YOUR HOME INTO THE GARDEN

series of compartmented garden rooms set within terraces and tied to a central vista. Each "room" was used to showcase a different type of garden, such as a planting of red flowers and foliage. Though the concept in fact dated back several centuries, Johnston's garden enclosures were called "entirely new," and even today Hidcote Manor's gardens are among England's most photographed.

Another Cotswolds garden that features "rooms" in its design is Snowshill Manor near Broadway. Designed by Charles Paget Wade in the early twentieth century, the gardens at Snowshill are strongly architectural, with a chain of terraced rooms built into a hillside. These steep, sloping rooms create an appealing sense of mystery and echo the architectural features of the manor house. Other illustrious garden rooms include those designed by Vita Sackville-West at Sissinghurst in Kent, England. There she experimented with a variety of garden rooms, including her famous white garden.

Today, considering the garden as part of the house is a practical way of gaining living space and creating a tranquil atmosphere, which is sometimes absent from modern houses. Garden rooms also offer a measure of freedom from utility. Though houses vary greatly in size, style, price, and other particulars, virtually every house includes

OPPOSITE: *A winding, informal path is both winsome and welcoming. More than just a path edging, this mixed border includes low-growing perennials and annuals that spill onto the path, small shrubs and ornamental trees woven in an embroidery of colors and textures, and luscious climbing roses and other flowering vines.*

LEFT: *Sometimes one fabulous piece of artwork can make the whole garden. This richly embellished urn recalls the grandeur of England's formal gardens. Planted with tiny, daisy-like marguerites, trailing, silvery helichrysum, and creamy, green-tinged 'Lime Green' nicotiana, the urn highlights a shady corner in striking fashion. A wall of white-variegated ivy, old-fashioned foxgloves, and modern hosta cultivars with thick, seersucker leaves and gleaming flowers complete the picture.*

17

certain rooms—a kitchen, an eating area, a living room, and a few bedrooms and bathrooms. Each of these rooms is intended for a specific use—cooking or dining or relaxing or sleeping—and there's little choice involved. Outdoor rooms are much more flexible; they can serve any purpose you want, from alfresco entertaining to growing herbs for handicrafts. Borrowing from the gardeners of the past, you might segment your outdoor space into several rooms, each designed for a different use or type of garden. The possibilities are almost limitless—you might incorporate a potting area, a child's playground, an outdoor barbecue, or an area for entertaining a crowd. Or perhaps your tastes run more toward a white garden, a rose garden, a fragrance garden, or a Japanese garden.

Garden rooms also provide you with the option of working on your garden bit by bit. If you're on a tight budget you can concentrate on one lush garden room at a time, rather than trying to design and plant an entire landscape at once. Gardeners with little land or leisure time can create a garden room perfectly adapted to their available space and time, and plant lovers eager to try out different themes can be as creative as they like without risking a random effect, simply by linking very different theme gardens into a cohesive design of connected rooms. This concept has worked beautifully in the past and is just as fitting for today's gardens.

BRINGING YOUR HOME INTO THE GARDEN

Throughout North America, there are many regional variations in architecture, which are particularly evident in houses built before the Industrial Revolution. Most builders made use of local materials and constructed houses in keeping with the climate, while immigrants brought with them the architectural styles and building methods common in their own countries. Thus, adobe houses proliferated in the Spanish-settled Southwest, while wood-framed houses with steep roofs that shed snow were popular in Canada and New England. Toward the end of the nineteenth century, mass-produced nails, hardware, and other building materials became widely available, as did published building plans and periodicals filled with advice on architecture and building methods.

By the middle of the twentieth century, houses in a whole range of styles were being built all across the continent with little regional adjustment. Some are modeled in a distinctive style such as Victorian, Georgian, Neo-Tudor, Greek Revival, Colonial, or Cape Cod, while many others have no clear architectural style.

When designing garden rooms for a house fashioned in a specific architectural style, choose materials common to the period and a garden plan that blends with the architecture of the house. You might do a bit of research into the garden style of the period, or you may want to interpret the style more loosely, adding garden elements that seem to have the same "feel" as the house. A cobblestone path might look just right in the garden of a Colonial-style house, for instance, while a split-rail fence or a redwood pergola would enhance the garden of a rustic cabin.

Marble statuary, imposing wrought-iron gates, and geometric planting beds suit more formal houses and landscapes.

If your house does not fit into a particular period or style, assess the "character" of the house and your interior decorating scheme—is it simple and spare, with clean lines and neutral colors, or is it plush and comfy, filled with patterned fabrics and country detailing? Whatever your style, extend it to your landscape. Remember that the interior rooms should segue smoothly to the outdoor ones. The process of designing and furnishing your outdoor space should be the same as that used for designing and furnishing the rest of your home. An ultra-modern house would look unnatural if it was furnished with large, dark, heavy pieces of Victorian furniture, just as a small-roomed Victorian house would look odd furnished with sleek glass and chrome pieces.

Carry signature features, colors, or materials used in the house through to your outdoor rooms. Distinctive pillars at the front of the house might be repeated as the base a pergola, for example, while an arched entranceway could be reflected in an arched arbor at the back. A house built with native stone might feature a garden room with walls or paths made from the same stone.

A house's geometrical shapes may also be echoed in the design of outdoor features. An octagonal bay window in front would be beautifully balanced by an octagonal gazebo in the back garden; a half-circle driveway could be repeated in a curved deck or planting area.

Motifs used in the exterior or interior detailing of the house make excellent themes for garden elements: popular pineapple, sunburst, or shell motifs, for instance, can be repeated in walls, plaques, and statuary. If your house has unique, handcrafted architectural details, you may wish to hire a local craftsman to build garden pieces that make use of the singular design.

And don't forget the smaller items—tables and chairs in outdoor dining or conversation areas should also be chosen with the style of the house in mind. Painted Adirondack chairs complement a white-trimmed Cape Cod, while old-fashioned rocking chairs highlight the porch of a farmhouse. Search flea markets and yard sales, as well as garden centers and specialty catalogs, for pots, urns, and other decorative details that will enhance the connection between house and garden.

Finally, the plants themselves can be selected to match the style of the house—a formal boxwood hedge works well with the classic lines of a Georgian house, a collection of cacti suits an adobe-walled dwelling, and colorful flower beds complement a pretty Victorian. Some gardeners take the period garden quite literally, selecting only plants that were available at the time their house was designed or built. While this type of garden can be interesting to research and encourages the use of heirloom plants, keep in mind that many cultivars available today are preferable because they were developed for their disease- and pest-resistance, their hardiness to extremes of heat and cold, their tolerance of drought and flood, and their improved flowering and form.

With a bit of thought and attention to detail, you can create a garden room that melds seamlessly with your house, whatever its style or vintage.

ABOVE: Foliage in a tapestry of greens complements the exotic architecture of a city townhouse.

FORM AND FUNCTION

To many people, a garden is just a collection of flowers. A garden room, in that case, is a "room" with flowers in it. But no matter how beautiful the display of flowers may be, it is not truly a garden unless it serves the purpose for which it was designed and reflects the intent and personality of the gardener. Likewise, the most stunning garden room is a failure if it does not meet the needs of the family who lives in it.

But like the family, the garden room will, of necessity, change over time. Small plants turn into towering giants while others never thrive at all. The play areas that were so critical when the children were small become obsolete as the kids turn into teenagers almost overnight. Some of these changes will occur no matter how carefully the landscape is designed, but you can avoid many mistakes by looking ahead and planning carefully.

One of the most difficult things about planning an outdoor room—or a series of garden rooms—is figuring out what you really want and need. At first, you may think this is the easiest part of the process, but as you contemplate the room's potential uses and decide on a budget, you are likely to change your mind.

As you begin to plan, ask yourself why you are adding the garden room and what purpose you want it to serve. There may be underlying reasons that you aren't even aware of: yours is the only house in the neighborhood without a deck; you think that if you only had a garden to relax in your life would fall into place; you've always thought that a pond with a fountain was the ultimate in elegance. Don't discount those feelings, because if you ignore them you may end up with a garden that never feels quite right to you. Also ask yourself what you envision doing in the room. Do you plan to throw lavish parties or do you intend to simply relax with a book or barbecue with the kids? These considerations will, in part, inform the design of the space.

Take the time to browse through this book and through garden magazines that feature water gardens, decks, play areas, outdoor dining areas, and other garden elements you think you might like to have. Mark the photographs that most appeal to you, and then go back and try to identify what, specifically, you like about those pictures. You might find that it's not the plants as much as the neat appearance of the brick walk. It may not be the water garden that draws your attention as much as that one spectacular plant.

OPPOSITE: *This Spanish Mission–style house features a central courtyard that is expansive enough to serve as the family living room in warm weather. Arcaded galleries— wide enough to accommodate a table and chairs or a comfortable settee—surround the courtyard, providing a refuge from the sun's rays and shelter during rainstorms. The tall, elaborate fountain offers a pleasing focal point for the courtyard, and contributes the cooling splash of running water. Terra-cotta pots filled with colorful flowers and verdant foliage circle the fountain in a scene of cheerful extravagance.*

BELOW RIGHT: *Even a small city lot can be landscaped into several functional garden rooms. Here, a raised platform constructed of decking and surrounded by trees serves as an outdoor eating area. A path circles the platform to the back of the garden, while in the foreground, one set of stairs leads up toward the back door and another around to a side garden.*

OPPOSITE: *The dappled shade of vines trailing along a pergola makes the water appear both darker and deeper, adding a touch of mystery to an outdoor room that boasts a restful simplicity. What could have been dead space in this narrow side yard has been transformed into a miniature sanctuary. A single fountain breaks the stillness of the carefully planted pool, where one prominent piece of statuary and a few containers are the only features to embellish the minimalist design.*

24

Next, take a good look at the outside of your house—what do you like about it? The carefully balanced pillars and windows? The relaxed, sprawling look? The intricate brickwork around the chimney or the gabled roof? Make a note of these, too, and incorporate elements of the house into the garden's design or embellishments.

Once you have identified the type of outdoor room you would like—or at least some features you'd like it to include—think about the realities of your house and its lot. Do you have space for the type of outdoor room you want? If not, can your idea be modified or adapted to fit the existing space? Keep the purpose of the room in mind when you are considering the location for it—if you want to enjoy the sound of water splashing from a waterfall or fountain, be sure to site it close to the house or plan for a bench beside the water garden. If the room is to be used as a children's play area, do you want it close to a back window so the play can be monitored, or would you rather have the play area, with its inevitable noise and activity, further removed from the house? If you are planning a deck or patio for dining or entertaining, do you have sufficient lighting and/or electricity at the location you have selected? Is the spot accessible

Plants and structures that lead up to or surround an entrance can add beauty, an element of privacy, and curb appeal to your home. Unfortunately, they can also create an enticing environment for burglars. Even the safest neighborhoods have the occasional break-in, and while I don't recommend surrounding the house with laser beams and barbed wire, it makes sense to take some precautions.

Landscape lighting emphasizes plants and architectural features, but it can also provide useful security. Low-voltage lighting of the type that is easily installed as a do-it-yourself project is often used along driveways and entrance paths—these attractive lamps light the way for residents and visitors as well as deterring any unwelcome "guests" who might be prowling about. Porch and garage lights with motion sensors are extremely practical, although it should be noted that some are sensitive enough to be triggered by a bird or a nocturnal animal. If you routinely use timers for household lighting when you're away on vacation, be sure to have outdoor lighting turned on and off, too. Paying a neighborhood child to bring in mail and newspapers, and turn lights on and off in a varied manner can be worth every penny of the expense.

According to reports, burglars often follow the path of least resistance—if one house has a dog and the other doesn't, they'll choose the house without the dog. If one house has a security system and the other doesn't, they may choose the latter—unless they think that the presence of a security system indicates the presence of valuables that might be worth the trouble. And if given the choice of a house that is well lit and visible to the neighborhood, and another that lies in shadow, the latter is bound to have more appeal.

There are some precautions other than lighting the area that you can take to protect your home. Some plants are very attractive in the landscape, but due to lethal thorns or spiky branches, they are just not suitable for entrances or other areas where people walk or children play. But thorny shrubs can be an excellent choice where basement or ground-floor windows make your home vulnerable. A thorny, sprawling climbing rose or dense barberry, for instance, can be used to cover an exposed window on a garage. (You may have dead-bolts on the front and back doors, but most likely the door from your garage into the house can be opened with a kick.) Dense, prickly evergreens can shield vulnerable basement windows, although they will also block sunlight. Heavily thorned shrubs such as 'Crimson Pygmy' barberry are attractive, can be pruned or sheared, and when planted under or in front of windows, should prove very discouraging to prowlers.

27

OPPOSITE: A prickly juniper and an iron railing are effective barriers to the basement window, yet appear ornamental, especially when paired with the frilly blooms of pink petunias.

OPPOSITE: *If you are lucky enough to have space for several outdoor rooms, consider installing one at a remove from the house. This circular room, situated to take advantage of spectacular views, is defined by a stone balustrade and raised floor. Even though the hills and trees are barely visible in the distance, their shadowy presence adds to the impression of space and emphasizes the sensation of a room brought outdoors. Large planters with single, sentinel-like conifers frame the wide stairs, while a flower bed around the tree and potted flowers set along the railing soften the formality of this imposing garden room.*

to the kitchen for serving and clearing up? If you are planning a raised deck, will it block views of your landscape or will it enhance them?

If the outdoor room you are planning is themed around plants, don't forget two considerations that are easy to overlook: your work schedule and your regional weather. If you work all day long and will be able to visit your garden only in the evening, be sure to include landscape lighting in your design. It's not much fun to come home after a hard day at work only to find your beautiful oasis in a pool of darkness. Don't select plants that require a lot of maintenance, either—if you can't keep up with the garden, you will quickly tire of it.

Where you live should be a consideration, too—if you live in the North, be sure to include plants with winter interest. A garden room protected by a tall evergreen hedge will provide shelter from the wind but will also restrict sunlight. While northern gardens may need protection from the wind, southern gardens may benefit from a site that allows access to cooling breezes. In the North, any form of roof on a porch or arbor must be able to withstand the weight of snow, while in the South, shelter from the sun is a main consideration. If you live in an area with extremely hot, dry summers, plant flowers and bulbs that will bloom in spring, when it's most enjoyable to be outdoors. Or if you live where snow covers the ground until June, select later-blooming plants that will flower when you'll be able to enjoy them.

OPTICAL ILLUSIONS

You don't need to be a magician to create a magical garden room, but it helps to consider a few tricks of the trade. Magicians use mirrors, optical illusions, and sleight-of-hand to convince us that we have seen what we have not. By adapting these "tricks" you can make your garden room seem larger, wider, longer, or just more interesting and mysterious. Instead of white rabbits and playing cards, your tools will be color, light and shade, proportion, and perspective, all of which can be manipulated to create a scene that appears to be wider and deeper than it is.

While there is no design principle that dictates the size of a garden room, available space often limits the dimensions of the room or rooms. In addition, the intended use of the space may help determine its proper size: a room designed for reading or

BRINGING YOUR HOME INTO THE GARDEN

OPPOSITE: In a stroke of genius, the far wall in this courtyard has been painted a deep sapphire to increase the impression of distance. Several level changes and a variety of flooring surfaces—most notably shards of colorful ceramic set into concrete—add interest to the small space. Plants are kept simple, with the prevailing foliage accented by pots filled with cheerful summer annuals.

BELOW: Hot-colored blooms, including chrysanthemums, lilies, butterfly weed (Asclepias tuberosa), red-hot poker (Kniphofia spp.), and golden yarrow (Achillea spp.) glow in the foreground, while spikes of purple and blue flowers recede, creating an optical illusion that makes a small garden appear deeper.

quiet chats with friends will most likely be more intimately scaled than a room meant for entertaining a crowd.

City gardens and the garden areas allotted to townhouses, condominiums, and apartments pose special difficulties because it may be necessary to provide privacy and muffle noise in addition to maximizing space. Brick or stone walls enclose some of these properties, while others, particularly townhouse gardens, may be separated only by screens or wooden dividers.

Following are some creative ideas for making the most of a small space:

❀ Use color to create an impression of greater visual distance. This trick is favored by painters as well as prominent garden designers, and capitalizes on a well-known optical illusion: hot colors—red, orange, fuchsia, and bright yellow—appear to advance toward the viewer, while cool colors—blue, pale pink, and purple—seem to recede. Arranging your flowers carefully, with hot colors in the foreground and cool colors in the background, creates the illusion of greater depth in the garden.

❀ To make less appear more in any limited space, add lots of container plants. Small trees, standard roses, hanging baskets, topiary plants, and luxuriant container gardens can make any area appear lush and full. Note that pots and planters are particularly valuable in garden spaces where much of the ground is covered by flooring, as in a courtyard, patio, or deck. Today, pots in a wide variety of styles and price points are available, including pots of lightweight fiberglass cast to look like stone or terra-cotta. Urns and containers with architectural interest make ideal focal points at the end of a short path; they can also effectively draw the eye away from areas with little to offer. Your inclination might be to fill a small space with small containers, but consider instead a few strategically placed large containers with structurally interesting plants, a look that is impressive without being fussy.

❀ Include vines and climbers, which are great for maximizing space in the garden, whether they are trained up a wall, an arbor, a trellis, or a garden tripod. The world of vines and climbers is vast, and there is sure to be an ornamental or edible variety that suits your needs. These versatile plants can also soften the effect of a stark brick or stone wall, which might otherwise appear too solid and imposing.

❀ Install plants wherever you can. Some walls, particularly those made of stone, have pockets big enough to hold a bit of soil and a small plant; brick walls may have recesses built especially for this purpose. Plants suitable for wall recesses include tiny armeria,

BELOW: *Just a few square feet of garden space can offer lots of visual interest. These stately pots, perched upon a raised path's edge, are the same size, and thus maintain a sense of balance, but their slightly different shapes intrigue the eye. Scented geraniums, flowing over the containers' rims, encourage wanderers to bend down, touch, and smell the fragrant leaves and tiny blossoms. Alternating concrete pavers and cobblestone insets along the edge of the path contribute another element of texture to the garden, lending greater impact to this small space.*

hens-and-chicks, alyssum, saponaria, lobelia, candytuft, basket-of-gold, stonecrop, pinks, creeping Jenny, primrose, bellflower, creeping phlox, lavender, and thyme. Arranging containers filled with trailing plants atop a garden wall or affixing containers to the wall at staggered heights is another way to fit more plants and accents into a limited space. Also think about planting hardy specimens that can take some foot traffic between the paving stones of your path—try thyme (*Thymus* spp.), pearlwort (*Sagina subulata*), mountain sandwort (*Arenaria montana*), or carpet bugle (*Ajuga* spp.).

⌀ Lend drama to a small garden with water features, such as a small container pond, a cascade spilling down a wall of staggered depth, or a fountain set into a wall or a formal pool. The reflective qualities of still water add depth and mystery to a garden, while the gentle sounds produced by a fountain or waterfall are peaceful, and offer just enough white noise to muffle more distracting sounds from the neighborhood.

❷ Add ornaments that create the illusion of greater space. Victorian gazing globes, which reflect the sky and surrounding vegetation, have been recently rediscovered as charming garden accents. These accents are back in fashion after years of neglect, and can currently be found at most large garden centers in colors such as blue, green, silver, red, gold, and purple. The globes, which are usually displayed on pedestal bases, are available in different sizes, a few distinctive shapes, and occasionally in materials other than glass.

Taking the concept of reflection a bit further, some designers install mirrors onto garden walls, fences, or sheds, surrounding them with arbors, trellises, or simple frames. As in interior spaces, where this design trick is often employed, the view in the mirror creates an illusion of additional space. If you try this, do be aware that mirrors can extend their illusions to birds, which may fly directly into the mirror.

BELOW: *This traditional planter, known as a Versailles box, has been given an unusual twist with the addition of mirrored side panels. The mirrors expand the garden visually by doubling the view, a favorite trick of interior decorators, who hang mirrors to make a room seem larger. A low hedge of sheared boxwood replicates the straight lines and squared angles of the planter, which fits symmetrically into the corner of this intimate garden room. The geometric motif is repeated in the wooden trellis that covers brick walls.*

33

GARDEN ORNAMENTS

ardens and ornaments go together like summer and lemonade—you can have one without the other, but somehow when you put the two together, magic happens. Garden ornaments range from classic to kitsch, and from the supremely practical to the purely decorative. The best garden accents, from my point of view, encompass both traits: they are beautifully functional—benches, arbors, trellises, gazebos, birdbaths, urns, bee skeps or hives, and decorative gates are good examples.

To give your garden a unique look, choose accents that allow your personality to shine through while also enhancing the structural aspects of the garden by repeating themes or highlighting an architectural style. Take cues from the decor of your home and incorporate your interests into your garden through its ornaments. If you like to travel, you might pick up some eclectic garden pots or accents to highlight your outdoor space. If you are a nature lover, you can create a garden room decorated with ornaments that welcome birds and other creatures. The possibilities are nearly limitless, bound only by your imagination and the ornaments' practicality for outdoor use. And don't forget to consider ornaments that weren't originally intended for use in the garden—scour your attic and flea markets for pieces such as old sinks, milk cans, and even dining chairs that might be put to use out of doors.

Following are some ideas for ornaments that will lend your outdoor space a human touch, all in keeping with the spirit of the garden.

⊘ Some gardeners might include sundials among the ornaments that serve a purpose, but until I see them replacing their watches with sundials, I will continue to consider the sundial a pleasant excess. These pretty timepieces are quaint reminders of times past, and many are constructed so beautifully that they are works of art in themselves. You might look for one with an inscription to give special meaning to your garden, especially if you are a lover of literature.

⊘ As interest in gardening for birds, hummingbirds, and butterflies grows, more homeowners are installing birdhouses, bird feeders, and birdbaths, which are often highly ornamental. Do note, though, that many decorative birdhouses are just that; they were designed more for their beauty than for their functionality. If you want a birdhouse that

OPPOSITE: The soft, earthy color of a large urn blends well with the blues, greens, and golds of the surrounding shade garden foliage. Fern fronds rising around the base of the urn add to the impression that the piece has been sitting in the garden for a long time, while the large, rippled leaves of hostas and the spiky flowers of Polygonum bistorta 'Superbum' further the garden's claim.

BELOW: Bridges may be purely functional, or they may become the main ornamental focus of a garden. Here, a curved railing and worn planks arc over a dry bed of river rock in a stunningly simple tableau. A stone path heavily outlined in moss and edged by common bunchberry provides a fitting entry into the picture.

BELOW: *A pretty concrete birdbath nestled in a bower of spirea (Spiraea japonica 'Shirobana') and fragrant lavender (Lavandula angustifolia 'Munstead') invites birds to linger in the garden.*

OPPOSITE: Who could resist the sight of this small sprite sheltering himself from the rain, surrounded by lushly fragrant spikes of lavender? The footed (quite literally!) lead pot overflowing with scarlet begonias and the tiny silver-green leaves of helichrysum is a real find, with an emblem in bas-relief like the tiny twin of its cherubic companion.

36

will attract birds and harbor them safely, do a little research about the birds' needs before you buy—good books about fostering wild birds abound.

⊘ Fountains create soothing sounds and hypnotic images in the garden room, imparting an air of tranquility. While full-scale fountains may be prohibitively expensive, and also require a commitment to maintenance, tabletop fountains or small bubblers that fit into containers are ideal for garden rooms.

⊘ Garden ornaments may also provide an outlet for artistic or crafts-oriented gardeners. Handpainted pots and birdhouses, hand-cast stepping stones, grapevine wreaths wrapped with silk flowers, and even handstitched banners are all accents that express something about the gardener even as they decorate the outdoor living space.

⊘ A simple, serene space might benefit from Asian-style ornaments, such as stone lanterns, small bridges, bamboo water spouts, or large stones, which have symbolic meaning in Japanese gardening. Stones of various shapes and sizes may be used by the gardener to represent such essential qualities as life, water, and the soul.

⊘ Don't think that garden ornaments need to be expensive or elegant to have an impact. Whimsical items or folk art pieces can be as dramatic as their more respectable cousins. Feel free to showcase rusty garden tools, antique weather vanes, a child's wagon filled with blooms, old buckets spilling over with impatiens, milk cans holding dried flowers, and, of course, pink flamingos and garden gnomes!

If you have time, it can be fun to pick up treasures for the garden at flea markets, antiques shops, and estate sales. But be careful not to pay over-the-top for ornaments claiming to be original that may be good-looking fakes, or worse yet, may be valuable originals that belong to someone else (see sidebar A Hot Topic on page 38).

Trends in garden ornaments come and go, so select items that you will use and enjoy—or just enjoy! A rusted wheelbarrow planted with an autumn display of mums and ornamental cabbage may be as satisfying to you as an antique sculpture would be to someone else. Don't be ruled by the trends; decorate your garden with ornaments that bring back memories, that touch your funny bone, or that are just too perfect to pass up.

BRINGING YOUR HOME INTO THE GARDEN

"Grand Theft Gnome," "The Purloined Urn," "Stolen Pleasures"—these are not the titles of mystery paperbacks with lurid covers; they are the actual titles of articles published in mainstream publications in recent years focusing on the growing problem of garden theft. Public gardens, arboreta, and private gardens open to the public have suffered for years at the hands of avid garden visitors eagerly clipping and stripping foliage,

flowers, and twigs from ornamental plants, presumably to propagate at home. Many valuable plants have been nearly destroyed by the short-sighted thievery of garden visitors who would have a fit if guests in their own gardens whipped out clippers and baggies and set to work. A garden center in England reportedly took mug shots of two hundred suspected plant thieves and banned them from the shop after suffering nearly $80,000 in

losses. Still, most gardeners understand the passion for plants that apparently overrides common courtesy and good sense when faced with a public planting. It is an altogether different situation when valuable, and sometimes irreplaceable, garden ornaments are defaced or stolen from private gardens.

Homeowners may have steel-reinforced doors, deadbolt locks, motion-sensitive lighting, and a variety of security devices to protect the valuables inside their homes, but few consider the safety of property outdoors. Horticulture *magazine* recently reported that the theft of garden objects had risen in recent years from almost nothing to half of all the art stolen in Britain. In North America, a demand for antique statuary has caused an increase in thefts of decorative art from cemeteries across the continent—thieves have even targeted cast-iron cemetery gates.

From eighteenth-century statuary to lead urns to farm tractors, nothing in the garden is safe. The problem of theft from gardens has become serious enough that garden ornaments can now be insured and some items have been imbedded with microprocessor-guided tracking devices. Truly valuable statuary and artwork might be worth the effort of installing stainless steel pins that anchor the piece to a concrete foundation. To protect your own garden ornaments, display them in a part of the garden that is enclosed by fences or hedges and not easily accessible. Keep the garden well-lit at night and consider installing motion sensors. Finally, take clear photographs showing your garden ornaments from several angles, anchor valuable ornaments as described above, use engraving tools to mark statuary with identifying numbers, and if possible, insure unique or antique ornaments.

OPPOSITE AND ABOVE: *Because of the rise of theft in recent years, antique or valuable ornaments should be properly insured and should be set in a secure area of the garden.*

Chapter Two

EFFECTIVE
ENTRANCEWAYS

EXTENDING A WELCOME

PAGES 40–41: *Massive brick pillars topped with potted plants are spanned by an iron gate that invites visitors to peek at the garden within. This entrance exudes an understated elegance made less intimidating by welcoming touches such as the plant-lined path and the containers grouped at the gate like party-goers anticipating the guest of honor.*

42

OPPOSITE: *Even a tiny front garden can provide tremendous impact, given a little effort and a lot of creativity. The flower palette picks up the warm colors of the house, while a copper sculpture and brightly painted pot offer funky focal points and lend a sense of order to the friendly jumble of plants.*

F irst impressions are often lasting impressions, so it is important to create a welcoming entrance to your home or garden. Depending on the architecture of the house and the layout of the site, a house's front entrance can become a garden room in itself, especially if the area is well defined. Hedges or fencing that enclose a small front yard, a porch, or a beautifully planted entrance garden can all help delineate a garden room that acts as a sort of outdoor foyer, smoothing the transition between exterior and interior spaces.

The first thing that visitors to your home are likely to notice is the approach to the front door. Whether the entrance is from a sidewalk, street, or drive, the front path should be wide enough to navigate comfortably, level enough that it won't trip visitors, rough enough that it won't become slippery when wet, and designed with materials that blend or highlight the materials of the house. The path may be straight, on axis with the door (an arrangement that offers a pleasing symmetry), or a bit winding and indirect. Other paths may lead from the drive along the front of the house.

Generally, front paths are made of "formal" materials such as brick, bluestone, concrete pavers, pressed concrete, or even outdoor tiles. The gravel and loose pebbles so popular for garden stroll paths are less than ideal for a front walk because the material inevitably gets tracked into the front rooms of the house and becomes a nuisance to clean up. In addition, pebbles and gravel have a casual appearance that is better suited to the more private areas of the property. The exception may be for a country property, where informal living encourages a relaxation of the rules, and gravel or even wood chips may make up the front path.

Soften the borders of your path with low-growing shrubs, perennials, and annuals that draw the eye along the walkway toward the front door. When choosing your

planting, avoid thorny shrubs such as barberry (*Berberis* spp.), rose (*Rosa* spp.), Oregon grape (*Mahonia* spp.), and holly (*Ilex* spp.) for areas near a path or porch, as even compact shrubs can have enough thorns to scratch a child's legs or run a pair of stockings. If you decide to plant a hedge along the front walk, be sure to use compact plants that won't eventually shroud the house and give it a spooky appearance. Boxwood (*Buxus* spp.), low mounds of spirea (*Spiraea* spp.), 'Green Mound' currant (*Ribes alpinum* 'Green Mound'), distinctive hostas (*Hosta* spp.), fragrant lavender (*Lavandula* spp.), or lady's mantle (*Alchemilla mollis*), coral bells (*Heuchera* spp.), or compact daylilies (*Hemerocallis* spp.) are all suitable for path edgings.

The goal of the pleasant journey up the path is, of course, the front door. The door is usually the focal point of the entrance, and should express your tastes and suit

OPPOSITE: *The gate implies both an entrance and a welcome, transforming an informal border of lady's mantle and ornamental alliums into a memorable scene.*

BELOW: *This gardener has maximized the impact of a small front garden by dividing the space into quadrants and using low, formal hedges to edge the path. The neat flower beds are simply planted with perennials and bulbs; groupings of containers house pansies and taller flowers; and a few small ornamental trees and shrubs add depth.*

45

46

the style of your house. A classic Georgian door can make an elegant statement with the addition of a highly polished brass knob, door knocker, and kickplate, while a traditional wooden door becomes a beacon when painted in a deep French blue or a vivid country red. Consider adding wrought-iron hardware or replacing clear glass with stained or etched glass panes to give a plain door a distinctive look.

If you have a porch or a paved area around the front door, give some thought to the decoration of the space. Artful wreaths, wall plaques, or statuary add a personal touch to your entryway. Freshly painted porch furniture and colorful cushions or throws, accented by containers full of flowers, lend a cheerful air to this outdoor room. Do be sure, when decorating your entrance, to strive for coziness without clutter. You don't want the first impression to be one of disarray, and you certainly don't want guests tripping over pots, occasional tables, or other items.

Flowering vines or climbing roses can make beautiful accents in an entrance garden, but make sure that the trellis or arbor the climber adorns is strong enough to support the mature plants—climbing roses and wisteria need extremely sturdy supports. Other vines, such as trumpet vine (*Campsis radicans*) or Boston ivy (*Parthenocissus tricuspidata*), can be trained against the house, but choose carefully because these vines can damage some structures. Frame front windows with colorful window boxes instead of hiding them behind overgrown shrubs. Lushly planted window boxes are attractive and welcoming, and have the added benefit of giving the gardener a miniature plot to experiment with.

A porch or entryway is also the ideal place to showcase large, distinctive urns or pots. For a formal look, plant them with dwarf conifers, topiary, or standards and soften the edges of the pot with trailing greenery and flowers. Or you might opt for a more country cottage look, with pots filled to overflowing with old-fashioned flowers. Containers offer the perfect seasonal accent, as the plantings can be changed to high-light the passing year—the tulips and pansies of spring give way to Asiatic lilies and summer annuals, which in turn are replaced by ornamental cabbages and chrysanthemums in autumn. When choosing flowers for your entrance container garden, avoid flowers that are very attractive to bees, but be sure to include a few that will attract butterflies and hummingbirds to your front window.

EFFECTIVE ENTRANCEWAYS

INVITING FLOWERS

Nothing says welcome like a dooryard filled with vibrant flowers. But as any gardener knows, it is quite a challenge to design a garden that will bloom endlessly, even if you live in a region where annuals grow all year long. Fortunately, entrance gardens generally involve a manageable space, which can be tended a bit more intensively, given its powerful impact.

To kick-start your garden in spring, plant masses of bulbs, with pots of tall tulips (*Tulipa* spp.) and beds of nodding daffodils (*Narcissus* spp.). If your path or entrance bed is shady, plant hostas (*Hosta* spp.) among the daffodils so that the opening leaves of the hostas will hide the fading foliage of the bulbs. Brighten a shady path with pansies (*Viola* spp.), variegated shrubs, and easy-to-grow perennials such as lady's mantle (*Alchemilla mollis*), variegated Solomon's seal (*Polygonatum* spp.), astilbe (*Astilbe* spp.), foamflower (*Tiarella cordifolia*), and lungwort (*Pulmonaria* spp.).

OPPOSITE: *Any house gains instant character with thoughtful plantings. This doorway wreathed in romantic wisteria welcomes visitors with dripping panicles of fragrant flowers and delicate green leaves.*

BELOW: *Old-fashioned flowers elicit nostalgic memories of our grandmothers' gardens, which were filled with peonies (*Paeonia *spp.) and daisy-type flowers like the Shasta daisy (*Chrysanthemum × superbum*) shown here. Also consider other familiar favorites, such as old roses (*Rosa *spp.), tall hollyhocks (*Alcea rosea*), prolific cosmos (*Cosmos *spp.), and lots of spring bulbs.*

50

If a fence or wall frames your entrance garden, include tall species such as sunflowers (*Helianthus annuus*), spider flowers (*Cleome hasslerana*), larkspur (*Delphinium* spp.)—if you live in an area where they will thrive—or old-fashioned hollyhocks (*Alcea rosea*). Irises (*Iris* spp.), flowering tobacco (*Nicotiana* spp.), and peonies (*Paeonia* spp.) are all favorites from grandma's garden that won't let you down, and have flowers to beat the band. A note about peonies—don't worry if you see ants on the flowers, because ants aid in opening the blooms. Also, avoid transplanting peonies unless it's absolutely necessary; they are incredibly long-lived, sometimes as long as fifty years, but resent being moved. Check out single-flowered peonies, such as 'Krinkled White', 'Abalone Pink', or 'Burma Midnight' as an alternative to the traditional "bomb"-style balls of flowers, which may get weighed down and trashed in the rain. Some of the single-flowered varieties are stunning, and have a more Oriental appearance than the more common fully double varieties.

Morning glories (*Ipomoea purpurea*), cardinal flowers (*Lobelia cardinalis*), scarlet runner beans (*Phaseolus coccineus*), and hyacinth bean (*Dolichos lablab*) are annual vines that will quickly climb a tripod, mailbox post, or trellis (with a little training); the seeds of all three can be sown directly in the soil and are easy enough for children to grow. Zinnias (*Zinnia* spp.), four o'clocks (*Mirabilis jalapa*), cosmos (*Cosmos* spp.), sunflowers (*Helianthus annuus*), nasturtiums (*Nasturtium* spp.), and love-in-a-mist (*Nigella damascena*) are other fast-growing annuals that can be sown directly in the soil and will flower the same season. Starting plants from seed is not only an economical way to increase the number of flowers in your garden, it is also a good way to expand the varieties you grow, since you can order from specialty catalogs (see Resources for some good seed suppliers) that carry more unusual species and cultivars than the ones generally available at local garden centers.

It takes more patience to grow perennials from seed because they don't flower the first season, but if you can stand the wait, it's certainly more economical than buying containerized perennials. You might also obtain some more mature perennials by organizing a perennial plant exchange with friends and neighbors. Most perennials need to be divided occasionally—some more than occasionally—and very few gardeners are tough enough to throw the leftover divided clumps into the compost heap. If you have lots of daylilies, hostas, and alpine strawberries to divide, you may find a neighbor willing to exchange clumps of lamb's ears, thyme, tansy, yucca, or lady's mantle for your unwanted extras. If you don't wish to trade, consider offering your extras to a local church or school—they will probably be more than happy to take the plants off your hands.

52

BELOW: *Annuals do not come back year after year unless they are self-seeding varieties, but they do have the benefit of fabulous flowers that fill in quickly and look great all season. This simple walk of aggregate squares is transformed into a magical display by the brilliance of the surrounding flowers. Robust dahlias, cheery marigolds, and spiky salvias are the stars of this small garden. Notice that the plants are growing in raised beds, which allows them to spill over onto the path but reduces maintenance. Additional topsoil or compost can be easily added to a raised bed, making the soil there rich and nutrient-filled.*

Annuals provide cheap and cheerful color for an entrance path or garden, but there are many perennials that also provide a reliable show of flowers or foliage. Russian sage (*Perovskia atriplicifolia*), purple sage (*Salvia leucophylla*), various forms of yarrow (*Achillea* spp.) and tickseed (*Coreopsis* spp.), black-eyed Susan (*Rudbeckia hirta*), purple or white coneflowers (*Echinacea purpurea* or *E. purpurea* 'White Swan'), phlox (*Phlox* spp.), daylilies (*Hemerocallis*), pinks (*Dianthus* spp.), speedwells (*Veronica* spp.), lilies (*Lilium* spp.), gaura (*Gaura* spp.), blanket flower (*Gaillardia* spp.), wild indigo (*Baptisia* spp.), sedum (*Sedum* spp.) yucca (*Yucca filamentosa*), liriope (*Liriope* spp.), asters (*Aster* spp.), cranesbill geranium (*Geranium* spp.), columbines (*Aquilegia* spp.), starflower (*Boltonia asteroides*), pincushion flower (*Scabiosa* spp.), and hardy shrub roses (*Rosa* spp.) are just a few of the many perennials that are easy to find and easy to grow. Add some dwarf conifers to provide interest once the flowers have bloomed, and include some small ornamental shrubs or a stunning Japanese maple *(Acer palmatum)* to add structure to the planting area. Deadhead flowers when possible since it often encourages another flush of bloom, mulch the beds to retain moisture and maintain an even ground temperature, and keep beds free from dead and diseased foliage.

THE PATH LESS TAKEN

A garden path is not simply a route that leads from A to B. A path—especially one that is long and meandering—is meant to inspire a sense of anticipation. Where will it lead? What interesting sights might you see along the way?

But paths are functional, too, without giving up character, and may be boldly artistic without losing functionality. A path may welcome visitors to the house, lead children to a play area, or direct footsteps toward a deck or patio. Paths laid out on strong axes link geometric beds in a formal garden, offering structure to the garden as a whole, while winding, woodland paths can open new vistas and make distant garden areas accessible.

Bear in mind that a path must be practical as well as attractive. A primary path should be wide enough for several people to walk abreast, which is more comfortable than trailing up to the house single file. A broad path four to six feet (1.2 to 1.8m) wide can be effectively incorporated into a design, as long as the width is in proportion to the size of the house and the length of the path. A curved path creates a softer, more mysterious effect than a path that follows a straight line and features sharp turns. If a straight, formal path is more in keeping with the style of your house, consider a path with different levels, or create sections of path set in angular designs. When using steps or gradient changes to add interest, be sure that each step rises a safe height above the last, at a spacing that is natural and comfortable. Slopes should be gradual—take care not to create potentially slippery spots or abrupt level changes.

A primary path serves a distinct purpose and should be well defined, well designed, and well lit. Secondary paths (those not used to enter the home or garden) may be narrower and more varied in style and material. All the garden paths should have complementary designs, though, to keep the landscape unified. The materials that may be used for an entrance path are limited only by budget, availability, and the style of the house—wood blocks, sections of log, pierced or patterned concrete, bricks of concrete or clay, neatly edged sod, flagstone or cobblestone, aggregate pavers, or terra-cotta tiles are all possibilities. Keep both safety and comfort in mind when planning your path—visitors in heels may totter on a cobbled walk, while slick surfaces may be dangerous.

BELOW: *Paths that grace back or side gardens may create an element of mystery by winding about, changing levels, or leading to a hidden garden room. This path is edged with feathery ferns and neat mounds of strawberries. The soft greenery growing between the stones is not a true moss at all, but rather a perennial groundcover called Irish moss (Sagina subulata). It performs best in partial sun with soil that is evenly moist but well-drained. In summer Irish moss is covered with very tiny white flowers.*

BELOW: *Weighty steps give this garden an appearance of age, but they are in good repair and are wide enough and tall enough to make them comfortable to climb. Plants along the path show off bright flowers and interesting foliage while retaining their neatly mounded or gently spreading forms. While the path seems to lead somewhere exciting, with such wonderful scenery, the walk is an end in itself.*

Wide, formal paths call for more intricate and expensive materials than are necessary for ambling stroll paths—consider bluestone, granite, traditional clay brick, or concrete pavers in standard or cobblestone form. Less formal paths are perfectly suited for materials such as flagstone, stamped concrete, pea gravel, crushed gravel, neatly trimmed turf, or various forms of wood. Woodland or wild garden paths may be topped with materials such as shredded bark mulch or pine needles. Also note that materials may be combined—a path may be made of local stone set in pea gravel or crushed rock edged with timbers. Flagstone and bluestone can be set directly in soil on a crushed gravel base, or, more formally, mortared into a strictly defined path. Paths made of loose materials can be set directly on slightly excavated soil or, for easier maintenance, on a base of heavy landscape fabric that acts as a weed barrier.

To get started planning your path, first list the materials you find most aesthetically pleasing. Next, research the costs for each chosen material in your area (note that costs may vary widely from region to region depending on local availability), then cross out those that exceed your budget. Consider the remaining materials, eliminating any that would clash with the architectural style of your house as well as any that are impractical for your intended use. After finalizing your selection, you may want to be creative and install a path of your own design. If gradient changes, drainage problems, or design challenges are beyond your capabilities, consult a landscape architect or a landscape contractor. The former should be able to give you advice on engineering, aesthetic, and structural aspects of the design, while the latter should be able to tackle the actual installation.

A winding path can create a sense of mystery, especially if it leads to a carefully framed focal point such as a garden bench, an artistically planted urn, a rose-festooned arbor, or even a simple birdbath. Plan for focal points along the path, too—a cluster of bold canna lilies, containers set in strategic spots along the perennial border, a gazing globe, or a garden ornament half hidden by foliage. Paths that have not been mortared can be made more interesting with pockets of sea thrift (*Armeria* spp.), tiny stonecrops (*Sedum* spp.), hens-and-chicks (*Sempervivum* spp.), thyme (*Thymus* spp.), creeping phlox (*Phlox stolonifera*), or moss planted between bricks or paving stones. Be careful with moss in damp areas, though, as it can cause surfaces to become slippery. Paths that include areas with stairsteps look especially artistic with clusters of tiny flowers spilling down step by step.

A border of low-growing perennials planted along the path will spill over and soften its edges without making the path seem excessively narrow or crowded. Hostas (*Hosta* spp.) in assorted sizes are excellent choices for shady paths; other shady selections include lady's mantle (*Alchemilla mollis*), lamium (*Lamium* spp.), and astilbes (*Astilbe* spp.). For sunnier spots consider coral bells (*Heuchera* spp.), snow-in-summer (*Cerastium tomentosum*), lamb's ears (*Stachys byzantina*), compact 'Stella d'Oro' daylilies (*Hemerocallis* 'Stella d'Oro'), stonecrop (*Sedum* spp.), lavender (*Lavandula* spp.), pinks (*Dianthus* spp.), candytuft (*Iberis* spp.), cranesbills (*Geranium* spp.), and other low-growing perennials.

BELOW: *Fallen leaves weave a brilliant carpet across this gravel path, which offers a tantalizing choice of direction. If you have the space, incorporating a path that forks can be a foolproof way to add interest to the garden. The paths may separate only briefly, creating a small island of greenery, or they may diverge completely, leading to different areas of the garden.*

Chapter Three

DESIGNING THE SPACE

THINK PRACTICALLY

PAGES 56–57: *Nothing strikes the right note in a garden quite like a perfect piece of statuary or a stately garden ornament. A stunning accent like the urn shown here provides a strong focal point and a hint of history, and often continues the theme of the garden. This garden room, with its clean lines, straightforward gravel paths, neatly trimmed boxwood hedges, and understated plantings of fragrant herbs and flowers, invokes a feeling of classical simplicity.*

OPPOSITE: As you plan your garden room, consider its intended use, your budget, and the resources you have at hand. This delightful space segues from a shady patio defined by wooden flooring, to a stone-floored eating area, to a small walled garden. A wooden park bench, placed at a 90-degree angle to a house wall, creates a "wall" for the eating area, effectively separating it from the garden beyond.

Designing a garden room is largely a matter of considering all your wishes and dreams for the space and then winnowing them down to what you can realistically accomplish with your time, your budget, and your space. Before you install a garden room, or indeed any landscape design, take some time to review the plans and be sure the following considerations have been addressed.

◎ Will the design of the landscape blend naturally with the house and its neighbors?

◎ Will the hardscape materials, such as brick or stone, coordinate with materials used in the construction of the house?

◎ Is this a project that you have the skills to complete, or would it be best to hire a landscape contractor, brick mason, or other specialist?

◎ Will it be necessary to change the grade? If so, contact a landscape architect to see whether changes in grade and drainage patterns will stress existing trees.

◎ Will the work require heavy machinery in the area of existing trees? This will compact the soil, damage roots, and possibly eventually kill the tree or trees.

◎ Will hardscape features be installed around existing trees? If so, consult an arborist or tree preservation specialist for guidelines on protecting the trees.

◎ Will you be installing an irrigation system? Check with your municipality; permits may be required and licensed specialists may be required to check the system.

◎ Will you be installing landscape lighting? While certain types of low-voltage lighting can be installed with relative ease, many states require that line voltage lighting be installed by a licensed electrician.

◎ Have you contacted local authorities to have power and water lines marked before digging? You should know the location of water and gas lines, septic fields, television

BELOW RIGHT: *A small gazebo, outfitted with cast-iron café furniture and set only steps from the patio, is a serene spot for morning coffee. While garden structures like gazebos and summerhouses lend your garden room a new dimension, they also require good planning, and may bring up issues like building permits and contractors.*

cables, and telephone and electrical wires and have them marked before digging or allowing others to dig on your property.

⊘ If professionals are working on your property, have you checked that they are properly insured? Joe's cousin may have a friend with a chain saw, but if he is injured while cutting branches on your property, you may not only be responsible for his medical bills but may also be liable for a civil suit. Hire only contractors who meet OSHA (Occupational Safety and Health Administration) guidelines.

✿ If stairsteps are being installed, are they at a comfortable height and depth for you and your family? Consider installing ramps, a wide, level path, and/or a handrail to make life easier for elderly or disabled friends and relatives.

✿ If you are installing any type of water feature, have you considered the safety of your children, neighboring children, or grandchildren who might have unsupervised access to the water? You may want to consider a fenced-in pond or a container garden that can be closed off from curious kids.

✿ Have you considered how you are going to water all your new planting areas? Do you have a spigot, faucet, or hose point that is easily accessible for all areas of the garden? Some homeowners prefer to bury a hose, leaving the ends accessible. Another alternative would be to have additional hose points professionally installed at various places around the house.

✿ Have you or your landscape architect considered designs that would bring dead space to life? Spaces between the garage and the house, as well as strips of earth next to driveways or along the foundation, might be ready-made for landscaping as garden rooms.

✿ Have you left a place to store the hose that is hidden from the street? Hoses can be unsightly but they must be dealt with.

✿ Have you allowed for a shed, barn, or other space to store gardening tools and equipment? While you're at it, you might want to consider a greenhouse, a cold frame, a potting table, and any other items on your garden wish list!

✿ Have you planted the right tree in the right place? Pruning chores can be greatly reduced simply by matching small spaces with small-growing trees.

✿ Have you selected the best cultivar for your purposes? Many well-known tree varieties have been greatly improved and surpassed with cultivars that tolerate drought, resist disease, withstand heavy storm damage, endure muggy winds and hot weather, and survive the extremes of winter weather.

These are just a few of the things to consider before you tackle a large-scale landscape project. Don't be too proud to call in a professional if you have questions or concerns—most will be happy to help. Once these issues have been resolved, it will be time to stand back and let 'er roll.

BELOW: *Knot and parterre gardens, with their strong geometrics, are shown to best advantage from above, so consider installing one beneath a deck or terrace. What could have been an awkward corner in a small city garden is handled with grace and ease. The end of the short path to the corner is punctuated with a tiny trimmed boxwood shrub, and the presence of the walls is minimized by a magnolia tree and several leafy climbers. A whimsical fountain rewards visitors with its tinkling music. The lily-flowered tulips brightening the beds are a pale pink cultivar called 'Ballade', which features petals that curve outward, exposing the rosy pink center of the flower.*

61

FIRESCAPING

While some regions are prone to flooding, other areas, especially those with limited water resources, may be vulnerable to sporadic summer fires. In addition to landscaping with plants that tolerate drought conditions, called Xeriscaping, gardeners in hot, dry regions should consider whether the plants near their houses would hold back a fire or promote its spread.

Initially, it was thought that the only way to keep a fire away from a house was to build a sort of firebreak—a wide stretch of soil with no plants whatsoever. In some parts of California, for instance, flammable plants and landscape waste were required to be separated from the house by 100 feet (30m). This safe area was intended to give firefighters room to work and to keep flames away from structures. Apart from creating an unsightly appearance, the removal of plants often aggravated problems such as soil erosion. Gradually, some plants began to earn the reputation as "fire-resistant" and were recommended for use as foundation plantings.

When forty thousand acres and more than one hundred homes were destroyed in fires that devastated California in 1997, fire department officials stated their belief that many homes

BELOW: Snow-in-summer (Cerastium tomentosum) covers the ground.

had been saved because of their "fire-safe" landscaping. And California and the Southwest aren't the only areas at risk for fires: wildfires in Florida and the Southeast have recently become national news, and other parts of the U.S. and Canada are vulnerable, as well.

Particularly in regions where fires are frequent, it's essential to choose a landscaping plan that retards fire. First, you must know that different types of plants put homes at risk for different types of fires. Surface fires that spread along the ground are fueled by dry grass and other vegetation such as needles and cones from conifers, as well as low-growing plants. Crown fires travel across the upper canopies of trees and across rooftops, igniting foliage, cones, and roofing. Landscapes can also provide "ladder fuels" that encourage the spread of fire by providing steps for the flames to climb, leaping from grass to shrub, from shrub to tree branch, from tree branch to tree crown, and from crown to house roof.

Where a high risk for fire exists, consider limiting plants in the immediate vicinity of the house to low-growing, water-storing succulents, gravel and other non-flammable paths, or turf. Slightly further from the house, plant native and ornamental trees at widely spaced intervals along with low-growing shrubs, groundcovers, and lawn grass. The outside perimeter of the landscape may be planted with native or ornamental plants, spaced to discourage paths for fire to travel along. Select smaller, ornamental trees rather than large shade trees, and beware of underplanting with shrubs that could form a ladder effect.

While any plant will burn in a serious fire, some plants ignite very quickly and should be avoided in areas at high risk for fire. These include ornamental grasses such as Pampas grass (Cortaderia spp.), fruit vines, bougainvillea (Bougainvillea spp.), New Zealand flax (Phormium tenax), pine (Pinus spp.), acacia (Acacia spp.), juniper (Juniperus spp.), eucalyptus (Eucalyptus spp.), and cypress (Cupressus spp.)

On the other hand, there are succulents and drought-tolerant plants that are generally slower to ignite (but remember that "fire-resistant" does not mean "fire-proof"). It is important to note that even fire-resistant plants become a hazard if debris, such as dead leaves and fallen flowers, is allowed to accumulate, or if the plants are allowed to dry out. Following is a selected list of plants that are slower to ignite than most.

Aloe (Aloe spp.)
Alyssum (Alyssum spp.)
California poppies (Eschscholzia californica)
Crassula (Crassula spp.)
Delosperma (Delosperma spp.)
French marigolds (Tagetes patula)
Gazania (Gazania spp.)
Lily of the Nile (Agapanthus africanus)
Lobelia (Lobelia spp.)
Pinks (Dianthus spp.)
Red-hot poker (Kniphofia spp.)
Sea thrift (Armeria spp.)
Senecio (Senecio spp.)
Snow-in-summer (Cerastium tomentosum)
Stonecrop (Sedum spp.)

DESIGNING THE SPACE

SEPARATE GARDENS:
WITHIN THESE WALLS

I t takes more than different themes or color schemes to distinguish a garden room from a garden plot. Like rooms within a house, rooms in a garden must be defined. This can be accomplished by obvious means, such as walls, but it may also be achieved through more subtle methods, such as a change in "flooring," a shift of levels, the deft arrangement of furniture or other elements, a transition of theme, or even the addition of a roof. It is the sense of separateness, of enclosure, that makes a room seem safe and secure. To create a refuge from the world, a garden room should feel like an escape. It should be comfortable, but with an edge of mystery at the same time.

Perhaps the simplest way to separate a garden room from other rooms or from the rest of the landscape is to construct walls, either using shrubs to create a dense hedge—boxwood (*Buxus* spp.), privet (*Ligustrum* spp.), alpine currant (*Ribes alpinum*), holly (*Ilex* spp.), yew (*Taxus* spp.), or arborvitae (*Thuja* spp.) are just a few possibilities—or using hardscape materials to build a fence or wall. Hedges take a few years to mature, but once established, they need only pruning and minimal attention to maintain them. Different hedge shrubs can be selected to create either a low divider or a tall screen, depending on the amount of privacy required.

Fences are probably the least expensive type of hardscape divider, and are usually made of wood but sometimes incorporate iron, glass, or other materials. Fences can be relatively low, designed to delineate a space, or they may be tall and sheltering, intended to section off a private area (although local zoning laws may restrict the size and placement of walls and fences). A low picket fence, for instance, clearly defines a garden area while signaling a welcome with its open design. A taller, stockade-type fence marks the enclosed garden as a private space. Other types of fences include those made with interwoven slats, decorative open panels, split rails, vertical boards, closed boards, diagonal boards, and wrought iron.

If a fence is used to enclose the garden room, be sure that the material in both the fencing and the gate complements the house's architectural style. Repeat materials and patterns used in the construction of the house and outbuildings whenever possible. If the tops of the windows or doorways are arched, select a gate design that echoes the

OPPOSITE: *This towering brick wall might seem intimidating without the softening effect of lush green Virginia creeper* (Parthenocissus quinquefolia) *and billowing pink hydrangea bushes. In a marriage of classic and contemporary, a bench inspired by the designs of architect Edward Lutyens has been painted a soft lavender.*

BELOW: *A simple picket fence is a perfect choice for a traditionally styled house such as a colonial or a country cottage. Overhung with the nodding heads of scarlet roses, the fence becomes a romantic accent as well as the defining border of an outdoor room.*

arch, or install a curved arbor instead of a gate at the garden's entrance. If there are geometric shapes or signature curves in the house's architectural details, repeat them in the design of the fencing and gate. Consider also the style of the garden room itself—a Chinese-style garden, for example, will look best with a fence or wall constructed in the spirit of Chinese architecture. For instance, you might wish to include a round portal, called a moon gate, rather than a traditional gate.

Walls of brick or stone are undoubtedly the most expensive type of garden divider to build, but are probably also the most long-lasting and effective. These materials present an impression of permanence, and can also contribute an appearance of age, as if the garden has been there for decades, if not centuries. Openings in the brick or stone, mimicking windows, guarantee that visitors will stop and peek through, so be sure to have something interesting for them to gaze upon. Consider the view from outside the walls when you plan your garden, and create vignettes to charm passersby. If your walls are more solid, you might create "windows" with mirrors attached to the inside walls. This approach visually extends the garden space, while allowing the garden to exist as a world unto itself.

RIGHT: *Entry into this intimate garden room is via a moon gate, a circular entrance common in Chinese architecture. While many moon gates are simple openings in a wall, this one features pocket doors that slide back into the wall or pull shut for added privacy. Inside the room, minimalist features generally associated with Asian gardens inform the space. Smooth pebbles, low-growing perennials, purple-leaved Japanese maples (*Acer palmatum*), and an intriguing fountain all work together to create a memorable garden room with an unmistakable flavor of the Orient.*

While brick and stone tend to be more formal than other materials, walls made of these materials needn't be built in formal styles or straight, equidistant lines. Stone walls are sturdier if they are mortared, but for a more rustic look you might construct a dry rock wall, in which the stones are set like puzzle pieces without mortar. This type of wall invites plants to take root in the pockets between the rocks. Walls in a serpentine formation may be formal or informal, as the undulating curves create a soft, mysterious effect that entices visitors to follow the wall through the garden.

You may also want to consider less common types of garden walls. A ha-ha, for instance, is a wall that separates one space from another without disturbing the view with the simple trick of constructing a retaining wall in a ditch or gully. To create a different look, you might vary the height of your garden walls; for instance, a tall central back wall may connect to perpendicular walls on either side that start at the same height as the back wall but then move down in graduated steps.

Retaining walls may also be used to delineate boundaries, since garden rooms may be elevated somewhat above or below ground level to create an interesting flow in the landscape. If the room is sunken, consider adding wide stone steps to lead into the

67

LEFT: *Garden walls, particularly those that feature cutouts or interesting gates, give structure to a garden in all seasons. The Gothic arch and glass windows shown here provide strong character, the open door offering a glimpse into yet another wintry landscape.*

area and tantalize visitors with a focal point, such as a large urn or small pool, that encourages them to enter. Sunken gardens might feature retaining walls of native stone, old brick, or timber, any of which could be made more appealing with the addition of a built-in bench.

Garden rooms may be perfectly served by a carpet of lush, green lawn, but in some cases a more solid floor is desired. Flooring can create a sense of a room within a room, or may simply provide a practical surface for activities such as outdoor cooking, dining, or games. Bluestone, flagstone, brick, concrete pavers, slate, or local stone are all good possibilities for outdoor flooring, and may be used on terrace or patio, as well as for paths or other garden room floors. If hardscape materials such as these are too expensive, look to aggregate slabs, pressed concrete (which can be made to look like everything from cobblestone to old timbers), crushed marble, pea gravel, and even shells or mulch. If you are using loose material such as gravel or shells, you'll need to enclose it within a frame of brick or timber to keep it from dispersing.

For an unusual checkerboard effect, alternate blocks of aggregate with same-sized blocks of turf. This effect can also be accomplished by setting slabs of waffle-patterned reinforced concrete across sections of freshly graded soil, and then sowing grass seed over it so the grass grows up through the small waffle-like squares.

It is not necessary to have a roof on a garden room—the clouds and changing colors of the sky are hard to beat—but when you do want the shade or shelter of a roof, what could be better than a canopy of trees? If you have tall shade trees that overhang your garden room, or the patience to wait for them to grow, count yourself lucky. If not, there are a few things you can do. First (this comes before the spade touches the sod), you might consider relocating the site of the intended garden room to take advantage of any large, existing trees. It is much more practical to work with the assets you already have in place than to move large trees (which often don't survive transplanting) or to plant fast-growing trees (which, unfortunately, tend to be less sturdy than slower-growing ones).

Another alternative is to erect an arbor or pergola and plant it with fast-growing vines. This creates a beautiful sheltered spot with the appearance of a green "roof." A pergola may be either freestanding or can extend from the roof of the house. Garden rooms attached to the house can also be sheltered by a retractable awning, a large, removable tent, or an overhanging roof or balcony. The idea is to provide shelter—from rain, wind, or sun—without obstructing the view or detracting from the open air charm.

OPPOSITE: *A retaining wall of unmortared stone creates a secluded garden spot for gathering one's thoughts. Nearly hidden in thickets of shade-loving plants, including hostas, ferns, and jack-in-the-pulpits, are two pots, which lend a human touch to the scene. Flooring composed of stone blocks and small loose stones also civilizes the space, which would appear far wilder if plants were allowed to fill in completely.*

DESIGNING THE SPACE

While garden elitists tend to value everything British, there are uniquely North American styles of gardening to be treasured. Many of these, such as prairie and desert gardening, celebrate the vast resources of the continent. Others pay homage to a singular way of life, and few of these planting styles are more uniquely American than the garden rooms we create on our porches, decks, and patios.

The porch has been a feature on North American homes for well over a hundred years, though it experienced a decline for several decades in the middle of the twentieth century. But both basic front or side porches and more elaborate wraparound porches are enjoying a resurgence in popularity, and are frequently featured in newly constructed homes. More than a visual link between exterior and interior, a porch also shields the house from extremes of weather and provides some shelter from rain and sun. Perhaps most importantly, a porch can be a welcoming anteroom, decorated with hanging baskets and pots brimming with flowers, country wicker, and whatever else reflects the comforts of home.

Some porches are constructed as narrow galleries that are fine for displaying plants but less practical for daily use. If your porch is wide enough, make the most of the space by arranging garden furniture, rocking chairs, or a simple two-seater swing or glider to encourage conversation and meditation.

Decks are an American innovation of the mid-twentieth century, and are usually made of planking similar to that of a ship's deck but extremely variable in size, shape, and design.

Because decks are relatively modern developments, they tend to be found on newer houses or houses of contemporary style. Decks can, of course, be added to older homes, but be aware that the architectural styles do not always mesh. A quaint Victorian is certain to look odd with a modern deck cobbled onto its backside. If you aren't sure about whether a deck would be suitable for your house, check out the outdoor additions of similar houses or consult an architect.

A house constructed in a modern style is generally a safe bet for a deck, which can effectively increase the usable space of a house to a tremendous degree. A steeply sloped backyard can be reclaimed with the addition of a deck that has multiple levels extending out over the sloped area. A ranch house with minimal square footage but a large backyard can be transformed with a low deck that wraps around the back of the house. Deck planking dropped to ground level and extended into the yard is also an ideal way to connect the house to a garden room, potting shed, or a freestanding garage.

Little touches can make a deck stand out—alternating or angling the direction of the planks, creating built-in seating areas and planters, and integrating trellises, arbors, gazebos, or simple privacy walls. Many types of woods, stains, and waterproofing materials are available, and some are more suitable in one region than another. It pays to do a little research first, whether you are designing and building a deck yourself or having one built for you.

A patio, too, can be a garden room in itself, providing a place to relax with a good book or to entertain friends and family. This open-to-the-sky space may be at the back of the house or on the side, or may wrap around the house. Patios may be level with the ground or sunken, and may be constructed in any shape or size you desire. And don't think that the ubiquitous concrete is your only choice of material: patio flooring can be made of a variety of materials, including flagstone, bluestone, slate, limestone, sandstone, cobblestone, clay brick, concrete pavers, aggregate blocks, quarry tiles, or any of these materials combined with landscape timbers, pea gravel, and even mosaic designs.

The choice of hardscape material for a patio should be determined in part by what works best with the architectural style of the house—repeat materials used in the construction of the house, if possible—and partly by the people who will be using it. Cobblestones may look great and pea gravel may be inexpensive, but neither would be suitable for an elderly or handicapped resident, who could easily fall on the uneven surface. Some bricks and stones can become slick and mossy, while slabs of stone set loosely on crushed gravel can shift and become uneven. Consider whether to have the materials dry set on gravel or mortared, which is more rigid and formal but less likely to shift. Before installing a patio or terrace yourself, consult a professional to see if there are likely to be drainage problems or whether the patio will restrict the flow of air and water to tree roots.

And remember that decks, porches, and patios aren't the only architectural features that make the transition between house and garden. In various regions, houses and gardens may also include open courtyards, atriums (similar to courtyards but with glass roofs, usually vented), landings, breezeways, roofed balconies, or loggias. Whatever attached garden rooms you have or decide to add, make sure to consider these spaces as part of your living area and decorate them accordingly. By adding myriad flowers and foliage plants and a few personal touches, you can transform these practical spaces into glorious garden rooms.

BELOW: This patio combines concrete and wooden decking in a truly innovative way—concrete borders the area closest to the house, including a small pool, while wooden decking at a remove allows existing trees to remain in place. Potted plants smooth the transition between materials and create a charming garden above the ground.

CLASSICAL GARDEN STRUCTURES

Structure is an important part of any landscape design, since it is the structural features that will be visible in every season. Well-chosen and beautifully designed buildings and landscape features lend grace to the garden and may be useful in defining particular garden rooms and creating focal points. These features can also add height, a sense of permanence, or perspective to the changing landscape. Many structures called classical today originated in the gardens of England and continental Europe over hundreds of years. They have been refined and adapted over time and for different places, so that a general description may not encompass all forms of a particular garden feature or structure.

Allée—A long, formal, tree-lined walk that links different sections of a garden or stands independently. In Britain, allées are usually very long, majestic walks leading up to a house or garden entrance at a magnificent estate. The trees tend to be deciduous varieties that will ultimately arch over the allée to form a leafy tunnel or canopy.

Arbor—An arbor, literally, is a place shaded by trees and shrubs, though in common parlance an arbor is a support, usually arched, for climbers and vines. Arbors in various forms have been in use since ancient times. The size, style, and composition of arbors are widely variable, ranging from inexpensive wooden arches to elaborate wrought-iron structures. Some incorporate benches and even planters, while others connect parts of the house such as breezeway and deck. Since arbors have arched "roofs," larger arbors can also be considered shade-creating structures.

Archway—In reference to gardens, the term "archway" usually means a type of arbor, but it can also indicate an arch above an entrance door, an arch cut into a wall, or an arched roof over a gate.

Espalier—Similar to a trellis, an espalier is a form of latticework that is usually affixed to a stone or brick wall. It is then used to train a small ornamental tree, most often a fruit tree, to grow in the form of the espalier with its branches splayed flat against the wall. This method of training is said to produce the most amount of fruit in the least

73

OPPOSITE: An elegant archway provides access to the garden through a brick wall clothed with creeping fig (Ficus pumela). Through the wrought-iron gate (note its unusual Greek key border), the cheerful faces of pansies and the frilly blooms of daffodils beckon to visitors.

amount of space. The word espalier may also refer to the plant trained in that fashion and is sometimes used as a verb.

Gazebo—A summerhouse or roofed garden structure with windows or openings on all sides for viewing the surrounding gardens. Gazebos may be as small as a child's playhouse or large enough to seat several people at dinner. They can be square or round but are more commonly octagonal or another multi-sided form. Gazebos can be relatively rustic or extremely ornate. They are usually constructed of wood, but more formal gazebos sometimes feature iron or other metals and leaded glass.

Ha-ha—A chiefly British garden feature with a name of possibly French origin. It describes a low wall or fence that encloses a large garden, but is set below ground level in a ditch or gully so that the wall does not obscure or detract from the view.

Moon gate—Chinese in origin, a moon gate is a circular opening cut into a fence or wall that is large enough for a person to walk through.

Parterre—A symmetrically patterned garden that originated in France. Similar to a knot garden, but focusing on tightly trimmed patterns cut into boxwood, a parterre encloses a very limited number of plants. Clearly defined paths set off the design. Parterres were out of fashion for many years, but adaptations of the traditional form are back in style.

Pergola—A garden structure with tall colonnades and open cross beams overhead that provide partial shade while offering support to heavier vines such as wisteria. Because pergolas may be planted in long corridors, the term is sometimes used interchangeably with allée. And because a pergola is a support for climbing plants, it is also sometimes called an arbor, though in fact it is quite distinct as a structure.

Trellis—A trellis is a support with a lattice-type design that encourages twining plants to clamber up and over it. Other vines may be trained to climb a trellis if they are tied at strategic points. Strictly speaking, a trellis may be made out of wood, plastic, chicken wire, wrought iron, or even nylon net—it just has to be sturdy enough to support a growing vine. In a classic sense, though, a trellis is generally a large structure of wood or metal that is ornamental in itself.

OPPOSITE: *This six-sided, gingerbread-trimmed gazebo sits at the back of the property, providing a destination for visitors to the garden. The spectacular view of an evergreen forest is fitting reward for those who travel the path to its end.*

Picture a garden where flowers bask in shimmering sunlight... or a patch of dew-touched leaves and petals in lightly dappled shade... or a deep green dell hinting of mysteries in shadowed corners. Different types of lighting evoke different garden moods, and you can maximize your garden's assets to make the most of these changes in the light.

Perhaps most important in capturing the beauty of light is creating contrasts of sunlight and shade. A tall deciduous tree or a vine-covered arbor will cast an exquisitely textured shadow across your lawn or underplantings. Even a small garden that features no large trees can be dressed with a few smaller trees in large planters, which will throw interesting dappled patterns, though on a much smaller scale.

Certain plants, too, seem to highlight sunshine and shade more dramatically than others do. The finely textured leaves of honey locust, stark yuccas, distinctive Japanese maples, and the tall fronds of ornamental grasses are all effective in silhouette. Trees with gnarly branches, weeping forms, or other distinctive shapes can be pruned and planted in a way that maximizes the effect of shadows cast on the lawn. Think like an artist—consider Monet's studies of haystacks and waterlilies in different lights, in different seasons, and at different times of day. Then look at your plants with the same critical eye, and work with nature to emphasize the unique features of each plant.

Reflective surfaces like ponds, mirrors, and even gazing globes will also enhance the impression of light in the garden. Because these surfaces reflect whatever meets them, you'll amplify the light surrounding the feature. And mirrors not only reflect light but also give the illusion of enlarging the reflected garden.

In the evening, the garden room can be filled with artificial light that induces yet another mood. Candles and tiny, white fairy lights look magical when set about the garden, and are particularly lovely reflected in water. Torches also create a dramatic effect, as the shadows dance with every breeze.

If you want more permanent lighting, you might consider installing low-voltage landscape lighting. For the most natural look, avoid setting the lights in straight lines up and down driveways or outlining paths and patios. Instead, use the lights to highlight steps, corners, or places with potential danger en route to the outdoor room. Floodlights can be used to focus on interesting tableaux in the landscape, unusual garden sculptures or ornaments, or trees with structural interest. Also consider placing a few spotlights in trees, aiming down through the leaves to create interesting haloes of light and shadow. Setting a spotlight in the ground shining upward can be a dramatic way to highlight ornamental bark or distinctive branching, particularly if there is a wall behind the tree or shrub to enhance the shadows.

There are some drawbacks to low-voltage lighting, mainly that it is short-lived, with materials and wiring prone to weather-related damage and frequent breakdowns. While improved low-voltage lighting is available at a slightly higher price, the very best landscape lighting features line voltage, which

76

must be installed by a licensed professional. Line voltage is more permanent than low-voltage lighting, and because of the higher voltage it provides more power and brighter lights. The style and features vary considerably, and while prices vary from company to company and region to region, complete installation costs in the $10,000 to $100,000 range are conceivable. This type of lighting can be installed by landscape contractors or lighting specialists under the supervision of a licensed electrician, but note that specific regulations may vary by state and municipality.

Whether you install landscape lighting yourself or hire someone to do it for you, make sure that the lighting is not placed too close to plants. Low-wattage lamps should not affect plant growth, but high-intensity lights or mercury vapor lamps could seriously burn a plant. These and other high-wattage lights that are left on for long periods can encourage growth during times when plants are normally dormant, making them vulnerable to damage. In extreme instances, long, regular exposure to bright lights at night can have a negative effect on a plant's flowering cycle.

Creating light and shadow artificially with landscape lighting requires the eye of an artist as well as the skill of an electrician. A lighting expert or landscape designer can demonstrate the different effects created by various lighting techniques, but you can experiment yourself simply by observing the light shining through plants and shadows cast by structures in the world around you. As you become more attuned to the changes in the light hour by hour and day by day, you'll find a wealth of inspiration for creating contrasts of light and shadow in your own garden room.

BELOW: Gazing globes, popular in Victorian times, are today enjoying a comeback. Besides the impact of color, the strongest feature of a gazing globe is its ability to reflect the surrounding landscape, thus multiplying the garden's beauties.

DESIGNING THE SPACE

CHANGING THE GRADE

Depending on where you are gardening, you may be struggling with steep, rugged slopes or a flat, monotonous field. There are good points and bad points about both. A slope adds visual interest and opens up exciting possibilities for rock gardens and multi-level decks or terraces, though creating these features could be challenging, depending on the degree of the slope. A flat site is certainly easier to work with but often lacks the interest of sites with level changes. Just remember that one definition of a gardener is someone who tries to improve upon nature, so don't hesitate to get out there and change the features you don't like. Is your garden too hilly and full of rocks? Build a raised bed above the rocky soil. Is it far too flat for your tastes? Install a berm or a series of berms, or bring in truckloads of soil to create your own hilly contours.

Before altering the existing grade of the land, however, be sure to consult a landscape contractor. Changing the grade or contours of the soil, adding berms or raised beds, or even lowering the soil level by installing a pond or sunken garden can cause dramatic changes in the drainage patterns of the surrounding landscape. Established trees, in particular, are very susceptible to changes in grade or moisture levels related to drainage, to changes in available light, air flow, soil level, and to compaction of the soil by heavy machinery. When any of these conditions exist, be sure to have valuable trees protected by experienced contractors and professional arborists. Even though mature landscape trees are increasing acknowledged by insurance companies as valuable properties, a possible insurance reimbursement cannot begin to replace a tree that took several generations to mature.

Significant changes to the grade or contour of the landscape should not be made without a careful plan and professional advice, but these alterations may well be worth the time, trouble, and expense if the result is an attractive addition to your usable space, and an extension of your outdoor living room.

OPPOSITE: Dramatic slopes may require changes to make strolling through the garden easier. In this woodland wildflower garden, a set of wide steps cut into the slope creates visual interest and makes the steepest part of the path more comfortable to traverse.

BELOW: This gently sloping hillside, planted with fragrant thyme, adds depth and visual interest to the garden, but planting on a slope can cause some wear and tear to the gardener, so consider plants that will need little maintenance.

79

WATER GARDENS

Although the interest in water gardens has grown tremendously in recent years, many find the thought of creating or installing a formal pond with a fountain, a naturalistic pond surrounded by plants, or anything with a waterfall not only daunting but downright scary. There are all those momentous questions: what if I put it in the wrong place? What if I make the pond too big? Too small? What if the liner is too hard to work with? What if I can't hook up the air filter or the fountain? How will I keep the water clean? What kind of fish can I put in the pond? Will they eat my water lilies? What kinds of plants add oxygen to the water? Which plants will suffocate everything else? And the biggest question, how much is this going to cost?

The simplest way to approach water gardening is the same way you approached walking—with baby steps. Learn about the containers, the plants, the fish, the mechanics of filters, and all the other important aspects of water gardening by starting small and learning as you go. It helps to have reference materials and expert advice, but the best teacher is your own experience. Luckily, manufacturers who didn't want to miss out on the burgeoning popularity of water gardening have come up with several ready-made water gardens in containers of different sizes. Some even feature fountains and miniature waterfalls. Local garden centers and do-it-yourself stores may also have staff who can offer valuable advice for beginners.

Probably the easiest way to begin water gardening is to create a container garden. All you need to do is place a watertight container, such as a heavy-weight plastic tub or a wooden half-barrel lined with heavy-duty plastic, in a sunny spot and add a few aquatic plants. Depending upon the type and size of your container and on what you want out of your water feature, you have several choices regarding plantings or other elements. A tiny container may not support plant life or fish, as a small amount of water will heat up quickly, possibly killing the container's residents. But a small, shallow dish can make a lovely miniature reflecting pool, while an urn-shaped pot fitted with a small bubbler can contribute both an interesting accent and the soothing sound of moving water. A somewhat larger container—one that is two or three feet (60 or 90cm) wide and deep—will easily sustain a few water-loving plants, and perhaps even a dwarf water lily. You can add water to just about any pot or container, but if still

water is left untreated it will eventually become stagnant; instead of a peaceful pool you will have a mosquito motel. Some water garden suppliers offer biological controls that will check mosquito populations.

RIGHT: *Few gardens are blessed with a natural stream or cascading falls of water, but, luckily, nature can be manipulated by the hand of the artful gardener. In this garden, wonderful color and texture are highlighted by a rocky ledge, made slick and shiny by water spilling into the small pool below. Tall spikes of iris are balanced by the soft-looking needles of a prostrate sequoia and the shiny, round leaves of water lilies, while the tiny golden flowers of creeping Jenny* (Lysimachia nummularia) *are lit up by the grass-like shoots of variegated Japanese rush* (Acorus gramineus 'Variegatus'—*not a rush at all but a compact form of sweet flag*).

82

If you are lucky enough to have a natural pond, stream, or wetland on your property, make it peaceful and lush by surrounding it with bog-loving native plants or a few carefully selected exotics (make sure you are not planting anything that will become invasive—a good plant encyclopedia will note aggressive species).

If you don't have a natural water feature and have your heart set on a pond or pool, you can build one. Installing an in-ground water garden requires a bit more work, but isn't an impossible task. Preformed pools actually make the work fairly simple. These pools come in a variety of shapes, from round to square to kidney shaped, and in a range of materials, from plastics to fiberglass. Installing flexible liner-pools requires somewhat more talent in the do-it-yourself department, but isn't all that difficult either. Many specialty water garden suppliers offer kits for the home installer for both preformed and flexible-liner pools. There are also lots of books that give specialized information on planning and installing a water garden. If you feel completely overmatched by the job, turn to a landscape contractor for help.

Once your pool or other water feature is in place, it's time to plant. The proper balance of plants is generally accepted to be two-thirds coverage of the water surface, but this can vary somewhat depending on the specific conditions in your pool. Many water plants are best confined to pots; they'll often grow better and won't spread out of

LEFT: *A small bridge spans a slow-running stream. Its banks are thick with the swordlike leaves of irises, which will bloom as the season progresses. Bridges can also be useful to make the most of a boggy area or a low-lying section of garden that is prone to flooding.*

83

control. Water lilies (*Nymphaea* spp.) are among the most popular aquatic plants because they typically have a wide spread (in some regions they may even become invasive) and offer highly ornamental blooms. Following are some other good marginal (they thrive in shallow water) and aquatic plants for your water garden. Those marked with asterisks may become invasive under certain conditions so check with your local extension office before planting and be sure to contain them in pots.

Marginals

Arrow arum *(Peltandra virginica)*

Arrowheads (*Sagittaria* spp.)

Blue flag *(Iris versicolor)*

Cardinal flower *(Lobelia cardinalis)*

*Cattails (*Typha* spp.)

Dwarf papyrus *(Cyperus haspan)*

Flowering rush *(Butomus umbellatus)*

Hardy water canna *(Thalia dealbata)*

*Horsetail *(Equisetum hyemale)*

Japanese iris *(Iris ensata)*

Marsh marigold *(Caltha palustris)*

Pickerel weed *(Pontederia cordata)*

Sedges (*Carex* spp.)

Siberian iris *(Iris sibirica)*

Sweet flag *(Acorus calamus)*

Umbrella palm *(Cyperus alternifolius)*

Water mint *(Mentha aquatica)*

Water snowflakes *(Nymphoides* spp.)

Yellow flag *(Iris pseudacorus)*

Aquatics

Anacharis *(Elodea canadensis)*

*Fairy moss *(Azolla caroliniana)*

Lotuses (*Nelumbo* spp.)

Neptunia *(Neptunia oleracea)*

Parrot's feather (*Myriophyllum* spp.)

Ribbon grass *(Vallisneria americana)*

Water clovers (*Marsilea* spp.)

Water ferns (*Salvinia* spp.)

Water hyacinth *(Eichhornia crassipes)*

Water lettuce *(Pistia stratiotes)*

Water lilies (*Nymphaea* spp.)

Water meal (*Wolffia* spp.)

Note: Most floating plants, such as neptunia and water meal, are tropicals that must be removed before the first frost. Many gardeners treat these plants as annuals, composting them at the season's end and buying new ones the following spring.

Water plants welcome little animals to hide within their fronds, and even small pools can house a variety of wildlife, including turtles, frogs, toads, and certain varieties of fish—goldfish and koi are the most popular fish for water gardens. Fish are beautiful water garden ornaments, and serve a practical purpose as well. They'll eat algae and other organic matter, and most importantly will eat mosquito larvae. If you plan to fill your water garden with larger fish such as goldfish or the more expensive koi, you may want to arrange your pool to protect the fish from curious cats and determined raccoons. Since cats and raccoons dislike getting completely wet, you can discourage them from fishing by creating a pond or pool that has steep sides or high edging stones that hang over the water, giving the fish a good place to hide out of reach.

Highlight your water feature by giving it a place of honor in your garden. A simple path of flagstone, gravel, or even mulch can lead to the pond or pool, drawing visitors along and instilling a sense of anticipation. Command extra attention by framing the path with an arbor, or set a bench near the pool so you can sit back and contemplate the wonder of water.

Whether you are accenting an existing water feature or adding one, take time to learn about the necessary maintenance so the tasks won't come as a surprise. While the maintenance required for even an elaborate water feature is relatively small, you will need to be prepared to control plant growth, fertilize, top off the pool, overwinter plants and fish, and winterize the pool itself.

Despite the work involved in installation and routine maintenance, you'll reap huge rewards in terms of adding a peaceful ambience to your garden room. Whether your room is formal or naturalistic, cozy or expansive, there's sure to be a water feature that will enhance its appeal.

LEFT: *Water lilies are available in both hardy and tropical varieties, with a wide choice of colors and fragrances ranging from minimal to strong. The celebrated Queen Victoria water lily, native to South America, is of the tropical type. Perfect for the evening garden, this night-bloomer flowers from late afternoon 'til morning, scenting the air with its pineapple fragrance.*

LET IMAGINATION RULE:
PLAY AREAS

Play areas are one type of garden room where just about anything goes. You might elect to make a garden room especially for your children, or perhaps you'd rather just set aside a part of your garden room as a play area. Whether you plan to design and install the play space yourself or have a professional take care of the work, it is important to keep a few things in mind.

⊘ Know your child. Consider the activities your child most enjoys when planning a garden room to please him or her. A quiet child may love the idea of a simple garden room with a bench, swing, or hammock to dream on. A small gazebo can become a unique playhouse with a table for entertaining dolls or friends, or a more traditional playhouse may better suit your child. Some children enjoy gardening, and these kids will be thrilled to have their own vegetable patch or flower garden. Curious kids may like the idea of a secret garden within a dark yew hedge, with strange and unusual plants growing inside.

Adventurous kids may think a fort or treehouse is just the ticket, while others may prefer a skateboarding ramp, a flat surface for rollerblading, or a field for playing baseball or soccer. Boys and girls like to shoot hoops, and many kids would love the challenge of a great climbing tree. A traditional swingset, slide, or sandbox may be perfect for younger kids, while others may have more fun with some kind of monkey bars or jungle gym. For fun on a budget, set up a campsite in the play area, or create vine-covered wigwams for shady hiding places. Or follow up on a popular new trend—railway gardening. Taking the concept of miniature villages a step further, a railway garden combines the rugged geography and small-scale plants of a rock garden with a child-sized train running through it.

Let your child share in the design and creation of the play area, but don't become focused on any one feature—children grow all too quickly, and the play area will need to grow and change with them.

⊘ Avoid dangerous plants. Most parents are aware of the dangers of the great outdoors—sunburn, heatstroke, frostbite, lightning, poisonous snakes and spiders, predators, and such—and they pass on this knowledge to their children. From an early age kids are

OPPOSITE: *This extravagant playhouse offers plenty of opportunity for creative fun. Kids can use the tower to act out their favorite fairy tales or play house, or they may choose to simply run off energy clambering up the stairs and sliding down the wooden chute.*

BELOW: *It's hard to go wrong with strawberries, unless you or your children are unlucky enough to be allergic to them. Annual strawberries can be plucked and eaten fresh from the garden as long as chemicals have not been used on the fruits. Look for runnerless strawberries to keep them from spreading out of control, or select smaller-fruited perennial alpine strawberries, which make a neatly attractive front-of-the-border plant.*

BELOW RIGHT: *Highbush blueberries (Vaccinium corymbosum) are beautiful, low-maintenance, and productive when given the right conditions. The soil should be moist, well drained, and acidic, and the planting area should be lightly mulched; blueberries perform well in sun or partial shade.*

taught to put on sunscreen, drink plenty of water on hot days, bundle up on cold days, come in out of the storm, and avoid dangerous animals of all kinds. Less often do we teach our kids about the dangers of plants that may readily be found in woods and gardens.

No one needs to tell a child twice to stay away from thorny rose bushes or prickly barberries, but youngsters may be tempted to taste the bright red—and highly toxic—berries of a yew. Some plants may be dangerous just to touch; others may only be dangerous if ingested. Whenever possible, kids should be taught which plants to avoid. It may seem easy to tell a child just to say "no" to eating plants and berries, but if their parents grow fruits, fungi, or vegetables for the family's consumption, it may be harder for the child to discriminate between dinner and danger. Teach your kids not to taste anything unless you have okayed it, although this may be easier said than done. Older kids learn quickly but everything that gets into a toddler's hands seems to end up in his or her mouth.

Be aware of the plants in your landscape that could be dangerous to you or your children, and avoid planting them or warn them specifically about these plants (note

that the list is not all-inclusive; check with your pediatrician for local plants that should be avoided).

> Angel's trumpet (*Brugmansia* spp.)
> Autumn crocus (*Colchicum* spp.)
> Castor bean *(Ricinus communis)*
> Daphne (*Daphne* spp.)
> Foxglove *(Digitalis purpurea)*
> Jimson weed *(Datura stromonium)*
> Mountain laurel *(Kalmia latifolia)*
> Oleander (*Nerium* spp.)
> Pits of peaches (*Prunus persica*), apricots (*P. armeniaca*), and sweet cherries
>   (*P. avium*)
> Pokeweed *(Phytolacca americana)*
> Water hemlock—also called cowbane (*Cicuta* spp., sometimes listed as *Conium* spp.)

⊘ Make sure play equipment is safe. Be sure that every piece of equipment is put together precisely as directed, using the hardware supplied. Check bolts and screws periodically to make sure they are still fastened tightly, and check stress points to look for cracks or other danger signals. Wooden play equipment may need sanding occasionally to limit the danger of splinters, while metal chains on swingsets may need to be repaired or replaced if rust becomes a problem. It also makes sense to keep up to date with tetanus shots—accidents do happen, and tetanus is a lot easier to prevent than to cure.

Consider the surface of your play area, especially if it will feature tall climbing equipment. A concrete or asphalt surface may be well-suited for skateboarding, roller blading, or a basketball game, but not for the surface under a swingset or jungle gym. Grass may be soft on your bare toes, but if the soil under the sod is hard and compacted, the lawn may not be enough to cushion a fall. Also, grass under a swing will quickly turn into a hollowed out puddle of mud or dust. Mulch will do the trick, but not just any mulch (some may encourage the growth of airborne molds, while others may attract unwanted bugs). Several types of commercially processed mulch have been created specifically for playground use; you need not be too fussy if your play area is small, but a large play area may benefit from the more expensive playground mulch. Schools

BELOW: *The bell-like flowers of old-fashioned foxgloves* (Digitalis purpurea) *are enchanting, and they thrive in shady or woodland gardens, but remove these plants from children's or kitchen gardens. While digitalis has beneficial medicinal uses, ingesting it in plant form can be fatal.*

often use pea gravel on playgrounds, which sounds as if it would be painful to land on. To make gravel effective as a cushion, confine it inside a frame of landscape timbers and keep it to a depth of about eight to ten inches (20 to 25cm). The most expensive type of playground surface—rubberized tiles made from recycled tires and other products—is quickly gaining popularity. These are undoubtedly effective, but they do require an underground drainage system, which adds substantially to the cost.

Remember that no matter how safe the play area, younger children will always need adult supervision.

⊘ Be prepared for bee stings. Bees, wasps, and hornets have a nasty sting that, in most cases, turns into a small, raised, red welt that may hurt or itch. An ice pack and Benadryl may suffice to "make it better." An estimated 3 percent of the population suffers more severe allergic reactions, though, from severe swelling to difficulty breathing to anaphylactic shock, which can result in death if not treated immediately. If a child or adult in your household or circle of friends is known to suffer from a severe allergy, keep a prescription bee sting kit containing antihistamines and pre-loaded shots of epinephrine close at hand; minutes can mean life or death. A series of desensitizing shots can often protect against allergic reactions for years.

To reduce the risk of being stung by a bee, remind kids to stand still if a bee buzzes around them, rather than swatting at it, since bees tend to sting if they feel threatened. Bees may become more aggressive after a heavy rain, so be cautious venturing back into the garden. Also, it may be true that "you can't fool Mother Nature," but you can easily fool a bee. Brightly colored clothing, colorful floral designs, and soaps and perfumes with flowery fragrances can have the little stingers making a beeline to you or your kids. Bees are said to be attracted primarily to blue and purple, followed by yellow and orange.

Many gardeners are eager to attract bees to their gardens, planting flowers that will lure them and providing water and shelter, often old or dead trees. Use reverse psychology to limit the number of bees in your garden—avoiding blue and purple flowers, as well as plants that are very fragrant.

In addition to bee stings, the bites or stings of scorpions, black widow spiders, brown recluse spiders, fire ants, ticks, and other insects should be examined by your child's pediatrician. Whenever it is possible and safe to do so, kill the insect and bag it for identification.

90

OPPOSITE: *A stunning gazebo, set within an informal garden of lilies and other fragrant flowers, is a perfect spot to dream away an afternoon—unless you're allergic to bee stings. If you or your child is allergic, you might limit the number of heavily fragrant plants you choose, particularly for sitting areas and along paths.*

PLAY AREAS AND PETS

What could be more heartwarming than the sight of kids playing with their pets? Despite the popular image of dogs and cats as garden marauders, ripping up gardens and savaging songbirds, many gardeners and their pets have found ways to live together peacefully. Commonsense precautions are all-important when it comes to pets; if you are hot and irritable after weeding for an hour in the baking sun, your dog or cat will probably be equally cranky. If your animals are somewhat shy, don't expect them to be thrilled by a garden full of screaming children. When you put kids and pets outdoors, there is always the possibility that they will come in contact with each other in an undesirable manner, that they will come in contact with a problem plant, or that they will be exposed to unpleasant, sometimes dangerous, pests and bacteria.

If your pets tend to ignore plants as food objects, you may be able to plant whatever you wish. But if your pets munch on anything in sight—my own dog enjoys eating mulch and gravel as much as her dog food—then stay tuned to the following list of plants that have proven toxic to animals (check with your vet for a list of problem plants specific to your region).

*Bloodroot (*Sanguinaria canadensis*)*
*Bouncing Bet (*Saponaria officinalis*)*
*Buttercup (*Ranunculus spp.*)*
*Common milkweed (*Asclepias spp.*)*

*Daffodils (*Narcissus spp.*)*
*English ivy (*Hedera helix*)*
*Hydrangeas (*Hydrangea spp.*)*
*Japanese yew (*Taxus spp.*)*
*Lantana (*Lantana camera*)*
*Foxglove (*Digitalis purpurea*)*
*Purple mint (*Perilla frutescens*)*
*Tulips (*Tulipa spp.*)*
*White snakeroot (*Eupatorium rugosum*)*

OPPOSITE: A bent-willow chair is taken over by the family cat. If you let your pets roam in your garden, be sure that they are properly protected from fleas and ticks and are up to date on all vaccinations.

BELOW: Tulips can be dangerous to animals, so avoid them if your pet is likely to eat plants.

93

Chapter Four

PLANTS FOR GARDEN ROOMS

A HERITAGE OF HEDGES

PAGES 94-95: *Architectural features such as arbors, trellises, and pergolas can offer gardeners vertical space for growing plants as well as interesting accents to the overall plan. This bentwood pergola has been trained with climbing roses and vining plants to create an enchantingly shady tunnel. Along the walkway appears an array of ferns and other shade-loving plants, which have been allowed to encroach on the path.*

OPPOSITE: *Neatly trimmed low hedges of boxwood are here used to create a series of small enclosed gardens. Brick paths, the somewhat meandering hedges, and a variety of interesting plantings, from sedums to roses, encourage wandering in a walled city garden that might otherwise have seemed too small for strolling.*

P erhaps the best place to start a discussion of plants for garden rooms is with hedges, which can be integral in creating a room apart from other garden spaces. In North America, our definition of a hedge is clear—it's a neatly clipped row of densely branched shrubs that forms an enclosure or barrier. Occasionally, we extend our definition to include lines of shrubs allowed to grow according to their natural habit. But hedges have not always been so narrowly defined. In medieval Britain, hedges looked nothing like our clipped walls of box or yew; in fact, at that time hedges were generally constructed out of dead hedge materials such as brush, stakes, and even stones. Occasionally, shrubs were dug from neighboring forests and planted into hedges. There is no clear record that indicates when live hedges, primarily English hawthorn (*Crataegus monogyna*), became more common than dead hedges; by Chaucer's time, though, live hedges were firmly established, although dead hedges were still in use.

At one time, hedges were used mainly to create enclosures for crops and farm animals, and to define property lines and political borders. Today, though, urban and suburban hedges largely reflect a passion for privacy. In an era when houses are built within speaking distance of each other, these natural screens create a sense of retreat and effectively muffle the noise of passing people and traffic. Hedges are also used to define garden rooms or set boundaries, to create a design (as in a maze or knot garden), to edge a path, or to separate one part of the landscape from another.

A hedge may be as low as one or two feet (30 or 60cm), like the boxwood hedges that commonly outline knot gardens, or as tall as one hundred feet (30.5m), like towering hedges of Leyland cypress. In addition to the traditional British hedge, hawthorn, the following trees and shrubs have long been found in traditional hedgerows:

PLANTS FOR GARDEN ROOMS

Buckthorn (*Rhamnus cathartica*)

Common European ash (*Fraxinus excelsior*)

Dog-rose or briar rose (*Rosa canina*)

Elder (*Sambucus nigra*)

English elm (*Ulmus procera*)

English oak (*Quercus robur*)

Field rose (*Rosa arvensis*)

Hazelnut (*Corylus avellana*)

Hedge maple (*Acer campestre*)

Hollies (*Ilex* spp.)

Ivy (*Hedera helix*)

Privet (*Ligustrum vulgare*)

Redtwig dogwood (*Cornus sanguinea*)

Sloe or blackthorn (*Prunus spinosa*)

Smooth-leaved elm (*Ulmus carpinifolia*)

Spindletree (*Euonymus europaea*, syn. *E. latifolius*)

Wild cherry (*Prunus avium*)

OPPOSITE: *Cunning cuts with the shears have given a topiary twist to these upright, conical conifers, originally planted alternately with lower-growing shrubs. While hedges are normally considered somewhat formal and sedate, topiary techniques can create eye-catching novelties or simulate architectural designs.*

BELOW: *Mention the word "hedge" and a handful of shrubs come to mind—boxwood, yew, laurel, privet. But there are many trees and shrubs that can be trained successfully into hedges, large or small. The tall beech hedge shown here defines a small, informal flower garden in a large lawn.*

Hedges hold a unique place in history, and they are sure to continue to play an important part in modern landscapes. For privacy, for structure, for establishing neighborly boundaries, for creating a sense of mystery, or for transforming a yard into a series of rooms, when it comes to hedges, the whole is definitely greater than the sum of its parts.

99

Knot gardens, because of their geometric shapes and emphasis on symmetry, are formal features that are aesthetically compatible with classic architecture and orderly landscape designs. But don't give up if you yearn for a knot design but lack a formal garden; the plan can be adapted for a more casual setting. In informal designs—cottage gardens, for example—knot gardens may be planted as perennial or herb gardens that are "informal within a formal framework," a style perfected by Vita Sackville-West at Sissinghurst. There, tightly trimmed boxwood hedges trace the rigid outline of the knot design, while herbs and flowers sprawl exuberantly within the boxwood frame.

A knot garden can be ideally adapted to fit almost any garden room—it can provide a formal outline for a kitchen garden, serve as a highlight at the end of a path, or become a focal point of a planned vista. Patterns for the knots can be reproduced from ancient geometric patterns or from lacework designs, or may be made up from your own imagination. Add height by adding topiary box or yews, standard roses or lilacs, or a dramatic garden ornament such as a large urn or container, a sundial mounted on a pedestal, or a piece of statuary.

Large-scale knot gardens require a network of paths to make them accessible to both gardener and visitors. Materials can range from formal brick or stone, to neatly trimmed strips of lawn, to artistically installed tiles or mosaic pebbles. In addition to traditional boxwood, the knot may also be outlined in golden privet (Ligustrum vulgare 'Aureum'), lavender (Lavandula spp.), lavender cotton (Santolina spp.), germander (Teucrium spp.), or compact forms of yew (Taxus spp.) or holly (Ilex spp.). Whichever material you choose for the outline of your knot, be sure to keep it neatly trimmed at a low height. Inside the knot, plant masses of tulips or daffodils in spring, and follow them with herbs, perennials, or annuals in summer, filling in with late-blooming perennials in autumn. If the knot's outline is composed of evergreen plants such as boxwood, holly, privet, or yew, the design will provide a focal point and important structure in the garden throughout the winter.

Since the overall pattern of the knot garden is its strongest asset, make the most of this type of garden by planting it where it can be enjoyed from an upstairs window or balcony. While the size of a knot garden is somewhat flexible, the garden will have the most impact if each side of the knot is at least six feet (1.8m) long. Also, bear in mind that knot gardens are traditionally plantings for full sun, and that most herbs and other knot garden plants perform best in well-drained soil.

OPPOSITE: Installing a knot garden is rather labor-intensive, but maintaining it is not complicated. Once the garden is established, the only crucial maintenance is to preserve the design's clean lines; plants inside the knot usually need only deadheading, cultivating, and fertilizing.

100

PLANTS FOR GARDEN ROOMS

UPWARD MOBILITY: VINES AND CLIMBERS

Vines and climbers are more than just window dressing for an entranceway or a garden room. A wall, trellis, or arbor adds much-needed structural interest to a landscape, and all of these features come to life when cloaked in foliage or covered in flowers. Versatile vines draw the eye upward, making the garden room appear larger. They can also disguise or completely cover an unsightly wall or building, and make even shabby sheds look positively sumptuous. Delicate vines like clematis (*Clematis* spp.) can be trained to weave through the branches of an old rose, complementing the blossoms of the rose and making the shrub appear to bloom longer. Fragrant honeysuckle (*Lonicera* spp.) will climb a fence and light up a shady corner, while the incredible flowers of the passionflower vine (*Passiflora* spp.) never fail to amaze garden visitors.

Don't be fooled into thinking that these delicate-looking flowers indicate a fragile vine. In fact, the breathtaking blooms of climbing roses (*Rosa* spp.) and wisteria (*Wisteria* spp.) spring from extremely sturdy vines and/or canes that require substantial structural support. Climbing and rambling roses possess long, arching canes, but the canes do not have tendrils that grasp a support. These roses must be tied or fastened to supports when young; with the help of the gardener, they'll eventually cover the support with beautiful, fragrant blooms.

Vines such as clematis may reach a splendid size, but the tendrils can be trained on something as insubstantial as a nylon pea-net or a piece of string. Give the clematis something to lean against—a rose bush, the post of a mailbox, or the pole of an outdoor lamp—and it will climb readily. Clematis, which requires cool roots but needs sun on its upper branches, can also be grown in containers and trained onto certain types of topiary frames. Like clematis, passionflower climbs by tendrils, but being a heavier vine it requires stronger support.

Other vines can be merciless as they latch onto a host, leaving a trail of destruction. While the twining vines of honeysuckle, silver lace vine (*Polygonum aubertii*), and wisteria aren't damaging in themselves, the size and weight of a full-grown plant—particularly a wisteria—can be enough to break a fence or topple a small tree. More dangerous to structures are the vines that climb with aerial rootlets, such as ivy (*Hedera helix*), trumpet vine (*Campsis radicans*), and climbing hydrangea (*Hydrangea anomala* subsp. *petiolaris*), or adhesive disks, such as Boston ivy (*Parthenocissus tricuspidata*) and Virginia creeper (*Parthenocissus quinquefolia*), which latch onto a surface with such tenacity that they can do serious damage. Brick structures

OPPOSITE: *Weathered double doors gain a splash of autumnal color with a fairly fast-growing Boston ivy (Parthenocissus tricuspidata). This tough vine can easily cover a large space such as a barn or an apartment house wall, and contributes winter interest with its tracery of branches and persistent blue berries.*

BELOW: *The rapid growth, robust nature, and pendant habit of Virginia creeper (Parthenocissus quinquefolia), combined with the undeniable ornamental value of its five-fingered leaf clusters, make it a worthy addition to garden rooms.*

103

will suffer less damage than wooden ones, but eventually the mortar between bricks may need repair. Ivy and climbing hydrangea are often planted against trees, but be aware that some trees can become deformed or even die as the vine takes over.

Some of the easiest vines to work with are annuals that can be grown from seeds sown directly into the soil. Morning glory (*Ipomoea tricolor*) is probably the best known annual flowering vine; other good annual vines include hyacinth bean (*Dolichos lablab*, syn. *Lablab purpureus*), scarlet runner bean (*Phaseolus coccineus*), black-eyed Susan vine (*Thunbergia alata*), and cardinal climber (*Ipomoea quamoclit*). Lesser known annual and biennial vines include cup-and-saucer

104

vine (*Cobaea scandens*), climbing fumitory (*Adlumia fungosa*), golden hop vine (*Humulus lupulus* 'Aureus'), 'Blackie' sweet potato vine (*Ipomoea batatas* 'Blackie'), and the tender star jasmine (*Trachelospermum jasminoides*). The true jasmines (*Jasminum* spp.) are plants for warm climates, so if you live in zones 8 to 10 you might wish to give them a try.

Sweet pea (*Lathyrus* spp.) is a lovely flower that has long been popular with English gardeners, but it does not perform well in areas with intensely hot summers. Other vines are so prolific that they have actually been outlawed in some areas—these include the notorious kudzu (*Pueraria lobata*), bittersweet vine (*Celastrus scandens*), which is poisonous and should not be grown where children will be playing, and the ornamental but incredibly invasive Hall's honeysuckle, sometimes called Japanese honeysuckle (*Lonicera japonica* 'Halliana').

Some outstanding but more uncommon vines include the twining ornamental kiwi vine (*Actinidia kolomikta*), which has green, heart-shaped foliage splashed with pink and white (plant both male and female kiwi for the best results); the delicate-looking but vigorous five-leaf akebia (*Akebia quinata*), which has lightly scented, purplish flowers; the hardy porcelain vine (*Ampelopsis brevipedunculata*), which has colorful berries that are attractive to birds; and the equally hardy Dutchman's pipe (*Aristolochia macrophylla*), which can be grown in sun or part shade. Exotic vines such as the spectacular bougainvillea (*Bougainvillea glabra*), fast-growing golden trumpet (*Allamanda cathartica*), and twining Chilean jasmine (*Mandevilla* spp.) have become easier to find with the increased interest in tropical plants.

Other ornamental vines and climbers you might consider are common grape (*Vitis vinifera*), Japanese hydrangea vine (*Schizophragma hydrangeoides*), climbing wintercreeper (*Euonymus fortunei*), Carolina yellow jasmine (*Gelsemium sempervirens*), and many species of clematis, including golden clematis (*Clematis tangutica*), Italian clematis (*C. viticella*), scarlet clematis (*C. texensis*), alpine clematis (*C. alpina*), sweet autumn clematis (*C. paniculata*, syn. *C. terniflora*, *C. maximowicziana*), anemone clematis (*C. montana* var. *rubens*), and big petal clematis (*C. macropetala*). Well-stocked nurseries and garden centers carry a good many of these plants, but some of the rarer vines may have to be ordered from a specialty mail order company (see Resources for some suppliers).

BELOW: *The formality of the entrance to this elegant garden is softened by fragrant jasmine vine (Jasminium spp.) wreathed around the brick pillars. While jasmine is hardy only in warmer climates, many cold-tolerant perennial vines are available, as well as a number of tropical vines that grow fast enough to be used as annuals. Vines can be used to draw the eye upward, making the most of small, narrow spaces, and can act as an effective frame for windows, doorways, and arches.*

105

A PLACE IN THE SHADE

Novice gardeners often look panic-stricken when confronted with shady garden spaces, their plans for a colorful flower bed skidding to a stop against an invisible wall of darkness. Actually, very few landscapes are burdened by truly deep, unrelenting shade—even wooded areas usually admit a few hours of dappled sunlight a day, and many so-called shade gardens get sun for as much as half a day. It is true that certain mature trees and conifers shade the ground so effectively that nothing will grow beneath them, but professional arborists can selectively remove branches to let in more light (a practice that should not even be considered by an amateur).

Instead of cursing the dark, celebrate shady spots by lighting them up with plants that perform well in part sun, dappled shade, or full shade. It is important to note, though, that a good many shade-loving plants are woodland natives that need soil rich in organic materials such as compost or shredded leaves and that require soil that is constantly and evenly moist. Some shade plants will even thrive in the sitting water of a bog, though most plants do not like "wet feet." Barrenwort (*Epimedium* spp.) is an exception, performing best in moist areas but also adaptable to areas that may be too dry for other plants, such as areas under a tree where there is competition with tree roots for water and nutrients. Even plants that will tolerate dry situations need to be watered regularly for several weeks after planting, until they become established.

Be very careful when planting under large, existing trees. Though we often picture tree roots burrowing in a straight line far below the soil, research has shown that the majority of a tree's roots stay very close to the surface and may in fact spread far beyond the outer leafline of the tree's crown. The tree's tiny feeder roots can be damaged by any kind of heavy machinery, even lightweight cultivators, in the soil within the root zone. When planting groundcovers, annuals, or perennials under trees, dig carefully with a hand spade and you will do far less damage to the tree in the long run. Remember that any herbicides applied to the soil in a tree's root zone may kill weeds, but will also be damaging to the tree. Also avoid adding topsoil or mulch more than about two inches (5cm) above the original grade of the tree. Any change in grade can be deadly to a mature tree. When applying mulch, instead of mounding it next to the base of the tree trunk, hollow out a circle around the trunk. This will prevent mice from sheltering in the mulch and possibly damaging the bark, and will prevent the mulch from rotting the bark. It also keeps water from slipping away from the root zone.

OPPOSITE: *Towering ostrich ferns* (Matteuccia struthiopteris) *arch over a stone birdbath, creating a grotto effect with their feathery fronds. Ferns grow beautifully in shade; just be sure to give them moist, rich soil.*

There are so many plants that thrive in shady spaces that a good number of books have been written on the subject, and if most of your yard is shaded, it may be worth checking out a few books specifically on shade gardening. But you may not want or need that level of detail, especially if only a portion of your garden is shady. The following section will allow even novices to start a shade garden with a few dependable plants.

Hostas and ferns are exemplary shade plants: they are extremely easy to grow and are easy to find in most garden centers. Ferns will eventually spread to form dense thickets in areas where little else will grow; once established, hardy ferns require little maintaince and may live for years. Hostas may be divided after a year or two, but other than growing to their mature size they are not in any way invasive. Literally hundreds of hosta cultivars exist, from tiny four-inch (10cm) plants to others over three feet (90cm) high and five feet (1.5m) wide. Hostas are available in a multitude of greens as well as in blues and golds; in countless forms of variegation; with lavender or white flowers; in fragrant forms; in many textures; and in many leaf shapes and sizes.

Many flowering plants are ideally suited for shady areas, although they do tend to be less showy than the flowers adapted for full sun. Astilbes (*Astilbe* spp.) are versatile plants with feathery spikes and fine foliage; they grow best in moist shade but will also perform well in sunny sites as long as they have adequate moisture. Many astilbe hybrids and cultivars are available, with variations in foliage, form, flowering time, and flower color (including peach, pink, red, lilac, white, and cream). Lady's mantle (*Alchemilla mollis*) is a favorite for shade gardens, and features wonderful foliage that cups the dew and delicate sprays of chartreuse flowers. Cultivars and hybrids of the late-blooming Chinese anemone (*Anemone* spp.), including 'September Charm', 'Honorine Jobert', 'Whirlwind', and 'Margarete', take a few years to really take hold, but once established will easily become a focal point of a shady garden.

Look for a wide variety of hybrids and cultivars among the lungworts (*Pulmonaria* spp.), foamflowers (*Tiarella* spp.), and coral bells (*Heuchera* spp.). Groundcovers for shade include Japanese spurge (*Pachysandra terminalis*), periwinkle (*Vinca minor*), sweet woodruff (*Galium odoratum*), golden moneywort (*Lysimachia nummularia* 'Aurea'), glossy European ginger (*Asarum europaeum*), Canadian wild ginger (*Asarum canadense*), bugleweed (*Ajuga* spp.), yellow archangel (*Lamiastrum galeobdolon*), and silver-splotched cultivars of dead nettle (*Lamium maculatum*) such as 'Beacon Silver', 'White Nancy', and 'Pink Pewter'.

Flowering plants for shade include monkshood (*Aconitum napellus*), columbine (*Aquilegia* spp.), lily of the valley (*Convallaria majalis*), bleeding heart (*Dicentra* spp.), foxglove (*Digitalis* spp.), and lilies (*Lilium* spp.). For woodland gardens, consider plants such as jack-in-the-pulpit (*Arisaema* spp.), Virginia bluebells (*Mertensia virginica*), trillium (*Trillium* spp.),

OPPOSITE: *This secluded bench invites garden strollers to take a moment to enjoy the serenity of the woodland scene. Filtered sunlight highlights the dazzling blooms of 'Sherwood's Violet' azaleas as well as the more subtle foliage of hostas and ferns. The verdant background only serves to enhance the brilliance of the jewel-like flowers.*

BELOW: *In a woodland garden, flowers are understated accents rather than the stars of the show. Rosy astilbe blooms are repeated here and there along a woodland path, giving the garden a cohesive look and introducing exhilarating color into the palette of soothing greens.*

bloodroot (*Sanguinaria canadensis*), mayapple (*Podophyllum peltatum*), cranesbill (*Geranium* spp.), and globeflower (*Trollius* spp.). Shade plants for those who like less common selections include golden hakone grass (*Hakonechloa macra* 'Aureola'), yellow waxbells (*Kirengeshoma palmata*), Italian arum (*Arum italicum*), bugbane (*Cimicifuga* spp.), heartleaf brunnera (*Brunnera macrophylla*), masterwort (*Astrantia major*), primrose (*Primula* spp.), Solomon's seal (*Polygonatum multiflorum*), yellow corydalis (*Corydalis lutea*), Dame's rocket (*Hesperis matronalis*), Christmas rose (*Helleborus niger*), and Lenten rose (*H. orientalis*).

Bedding plants and annuals in general seem to be mainly regarded as plants for sun, but in fact several familiar annuals perform as well—if not better—in shade. These include impatiens (*Impatiens wallerana*), wax begonias (*Begonia semperflorens*), flowering tobacco (*Nicotiana alata*), violets and pansies (*Viola* spp.), lobelia (*Lobelia erinus*), forget-me-nots (*Myosotis sylvatica*), painted nettle (*Coleus* spp.), caladium (*Caladium* spp.), and four o'clocks (*Mirabilis* spp.). Light up your shady spot with a few of these plants, sit back, and watch your garden grow.

GROUNDED IN GREENERY

Why is it that one of the most useful types of plant—the lowly groundcover—gets so little respect? Groundcover plants, once established, block weeds from taking over a planting bed, spread quickly without (in most cases) risking the health of surrounding plants, create a unifying appearance as well as textural interest, disguise the dying foliage of small bulbs, and grow in areas where grass often will not. Groundcovers require little care once they are established, although ivy, purpleleaf wintercreeper, and other forms of euonymus may need occasional shearing. Coniferous groundcovers may also need occasional pruning and trimming to maintain a neat appearance.

When groundcovers are first installed they should be planted closer together than usually recommended to speed up the "ground-covering" process. It may take two seasons or more before the groundcover is sufficiently established to crowd out weeds; until then it will be necessary to weed carefully around the young plants. A light application of mulch is beneficial, but avoid layering mulch too thickly, especially near the base of the plants. A starter fertilizer (look for a 10-10-10 mix) will help boost growth in the young plants. Like any newly installed plants, groundcovers should be watered regularly for at least the first few weeks after they have been planted. Until the groundcover fills in, use low-growing annuals such as impatiens, pansies, ageratum, or alyssum to give the planting area a more finished appearance.

If groundcovers have a problem, it is this: in order for a plant to cover the ground quickly and efficiently enough to exclude weeds, it must be a vigorous plant with a spreading habit. Unfortunately, those same features, while necessary in a groundcover, are also characteristics of an invasive plant—just what most gardeners don't want in their flower beds. Not all groundcovers are invasive, but a good number will become so when planted in good soil in an appropriate site. The more invasive groundcovers, such as carpet bugle (*Ajuga* spp.), chameleon plant (*Houttuynia* spp.), and bishop's weed (*Aegopodium* spp.), are best planted in tree circles at the base of lawn trees, with a sharp, spaded edge separating the tree circle from the lawn, or in beds that have distinct borders, such as those along sidewalks, patios, or driveways. Another alternative is to do some research in advance, and select only named hybrids and cultivars that are relatively easy to control.

Although many groundcovers do have flowers, in general the flowers are either fleeting or subtle. Even when the flowers are ornamental, gardeners generally seem less interested in groundcovers with beautiful flowers than groundcovers that will thrive under specific

BELOW: *This garden illustrates how a space can be clothed in greenery from the ground up, creating interest at every level. An effective groundcover for shady areas with rich soil, American barrenwort (Vancouveria hexandra) has attractive foliage and tiny clusters of white flowers. Above the barrenwort rise soft pompons of meadow rue (Thalictrum aquilegifolium); at the next level, the highly ornamental oakleaf hydrangea (Hydrangea quercifolia) is cloaked in fresh green spring foliage. Later in the summer it will bloom with large panicles of white flowers.*

conditions—boggy and wet, dry shade, heavy clay soil, extremely hot sun, poor soil. Following are some great groundcovers to choose from:

Alpine strawberry (*Fragaria* spp.)

Barren strawberry (*Waldsteinia ternata*)

Barrenwort (*Epimedium* spp.)

Bearberry (*Arctostaphylos uva-ursi*)

Bunchberry (*Cornus canadensis*)

Canadian wild ginger (*Asarum canadense*)

Chameleon plant (*Houttuynia cordata* 'Chameleon')

Creeping Jenny or moneywort (*Lysimachia nummularia*)

Dead nettle (*Lamium maculatum*)

Carpet bugle (*Ajuga* spp.)

English ivy (*Hedera helix*)

European wild ginger (*Asarum europaeum*)

Evergreen candytuft (*Iberis sempervirens*)

Fleeceflower (*Polygonum* spp.)

Golden star (*Chrysogonum virginianum*)

Japanese spurge (*Pachysandra terminalis*)

Lamb's ears (*Stachys byzantina*)

Leadwort (*Ceratostigma plumbaginoides*)

Lily-of-the-valley (*Convallaria majalis*)

Lilyturf (*Liriope muscari*)

Mazus (*Mazus reptans*)

Moss phlox (*Phlox subulata*)

Periwinkle (*Vinca minor*)

Purpleleaf wintercreeper (*Euonymus fortunei* 'Colorata')

Siberian bugloss (*Brunnera macrophylla*)

Snow-in-summer (*Cerastium tomentosum*)

Spring cinquefoil (*Potentilla tabernaemontani*, syn. *P. neumanniana*)

Stonecrop (*Sedum* spp.)

Sweet woodruff (*Galium odoratum*)

Thyme (*Thymus* spp.)

Wintergreen (*Gaultheria procumbens*)

Yellow archangel (*Lamiastrum galeobdolon*)

Daylilies (*Hemerocallis* spp.), especially the compact 'Stella de Oro', can be used as front-of-the-border groundcovers; lady's mantle (*Alchemilla mollis*) would also serve the purpose. Shrubby plants such as rosemary (*Rosmarinus* spp.), 'Gro-Low' fragrant sumac (*Rhus aromatica* 'Gro-Low'), creeping cotoneaster (*Cotoneaster adpressus* var. *praecox*), rock cotoneaster (*C. horizontalis*), cranberry cotoneaster (*C. apiculatus*), and Siberian cypress (*Microbiota decussata*), as well as many forms of juniper (*Juniperus* spp.), are also suitable for use as groundcovers.

112

OPPOSITE: *While low, spreading groundcovers are ideal for covering large expanses, low-growing ferns and compact perennials such as lady's mantle can be used effectively to fill in smaller spaces. Lady's mantle does spread, and benefits from occasional division, but it is ladylike in its behavior and most gardeners are happy to increase their supply of this useful plant. It performs well in shade to part sun, and the beautifully formed leaves are famous for capturing the morning dew. When in flower, as pictured here, the chartreuse sprays brighten up the garden without stealing the show.*

ALL ABOUT BULBS

hatever type of garden room you desire—a formal walled garden, a shady woodland nook, or a cozy outdoor sitting room—there are bulbs to enhance the design. While some bulbs bloom in summer and some in autumn, the multitude of spring-blooming bulbs are most valuable in the garden. The small bulbs that appear early in the year may seem insignificant when compared with bold summer blossoms, but after a long, gray winter each green leaf and tiny flower is a joy to behold. The later, taller bulbs such as tulips and daffodils hold their own just when everything around them seems to be bursting into leaf and flower.

Whether bulbs are planted in a groundcover carpet, naturalized in drifts, filling a bold container, or gracing a formal border, they bring an element of excitement to any garden. A truly valuable garden commodity, bulbs extend the growing season and offer forms and flowers that complement perennials and annuals. No plant is completely maintenance-free, but many bulbs require astonishingly little aftercare once they have been planted. Some, such as tulips and hyacinths, do not usually fare well after the first year—either returning smaller and less attractive or not coming back at all. It helps to think of those finicky bulbs as annuals—and if they do come back looking good, consider it a gift! Other bulbs naturalize quickly, creating a greater impact with each passing year. There are a few things you need to know to keep your bulbs as healthy as possible. Bulbs obtain nutrients from their foliage, so you should not cut the foliage back after flowering until it has dried up. Planting hostas and daylilies among tall bulbs is a good idea, because the emerging foliage of the perennials will disguise the bulbs' dying foliage.

Don't be stingy when planting bulbs—with small bulbs such as grape hyacinth (*Muscari* spp.), windflowers (*Anemone* spp.), snowdrops (*Galanthus nivalis*), and winter aconite (*Eranthis* spp.), a hundred bulbs would not be excessive, depending upon the space you are planting. Crocus (*Crocus* spp.), glory-of-the-snow (*Chionodoxa* spp.), species tulips (*Tulipa* spp.), and tiny daffodils (*Narcissus* spp.) look great planted in large drifts at the base of spring-flowering shrubs and trees. In a rigidly formal garden, straight lines of bulbs in military-style rows may work with the garden design. In most gardens, though, bulbs look much more attractive when planted in large bunches or drifts. If you want bulbs to naturalize in a lawn, be sure to remember two things: first, do not mow the lawn from the time the bulb foliage emerges until it has completely withered and died—if you do mow you will have inferior flowering the next year. Second, do not use any herbicides in areas where bulbs have been planted in the lawn. To plant masses of

OPPOSITE: *Pink tulips paired with a deep purple-red cultivar make a striking combination, especially when complemented by yellow daffodils. The blooming rhododendron provides a fitting backdrop for this floral ode to spring.*

BELOW: *Grape hyacinth (*Muscari armeniacum*) blooms in spring with small spikes of purple-blue flowers that bear a faint fragrance of grapes.*

115

116

bulbs, turn back the sod or dig the soil to the appropriate depth for the size of the bulb (when in doubt, deeper is usually better). Add a bulb fertilizer, replace the sod or soil (or cover with mulch), and water well.

I am lucky to live only four miles (6.4km) from the Cincinnati Nature Center, once the home of Carl Krippendorf. Mr. Krippendorf was a great lover of plants, and for fifty years he planted hundreds—even thousands—of bulbs each year. I don't know how many of his original bulbs remain, but each spring hundreds of acres bloom with winter aconites, snowdrops, crocuses, grape hyacinths, and daffodils, as well as other bulbs.

For years Mr. Krippendorf corresponded with southern gardener and garden writer Elizabeth Lawrence (*The Little Bulbs*, Criterion Books, New York, 1957); she wrote about their letters in a small book called *Lob's Wood*. One October, Mr. Krippendorf wrote, "I am getting on with my bulb planting. I don't think I have over a thousand bulbs left to plant.... On Wednesday, my day of rest, I planted seven hundred and ten small bulbs in the woods; two hundred and twenty-four large hyacinths in fifty-six ten-inch pans; and a hundred Madonna lilies in thirty-five 12-inch pots."

While I can't claim such vast numbers, I do make sure to plant lots of bulbs each year. My personal favorites are blue glory-of-the-snow (*Chionodoxa luciliae*), Siberian squill (*Scilla siberca*), 'Thalia' and 'Erlicheer' daffodils (*Narcissus* 'Thalia' and *N.* 'Erlicheer'), the peony-flowered tulip 'Angelique' (*Tulipa* 'Angelique'), tiny daffodils like 'Hawera' and 'Tete-a-Tete' (*Narcissus* 'Hawera' and *N.* 'Tete-a-tete'), grape hyacinths (*Muscari* spp.), and, well, the more I think about it the more favorites I recall. Give yourself the opportunity to be poetic—make room for some bulbs in your garden.

Chapter Five

ENTERTAINING ALFRESCO

STEP INTO MY GARDEN

120

There are garden rooms meant for solitary contemplation and there are garden rooms for parties and lots of people. Often, the types of outdoor rooms designed for entertaining are those attached to or surrounded by the house, such as decks, patios, terraces, and courtyards. This arrangement is mainly a matter of practicality, as having the garden room close to the house cuts down the distance the food, drinks, and dishes have to travel between kitchen and table. I remember years ago when I visited Versailles, I was bemused when our guide mentioned that the kitchens were so far from the royal dining room that the food was invariably cold by the time it reached the table. Who knows? That could explain why decks are so often built under the kitchen window.

Another practical reason for keeping the eating and entertaining areas close to the house is that the walls provide shelter if the weather turns chilly or windy, and the nearby house offers a place to run if it starts to rain. Garden rooms close to, or attached to, the house are also more accessible to running water, electricity, and lighting, which makes garden chores easier.

Having conveniences like electric lighting close at hand can also extend your enjoyment of the garden, since you'll be able to use the room into the evening hours. But don't think that lighting must be confined to floodlights attached to the house (especially as many nowadays are equipped with motion sensors that make the lights go on and off in an unnerving manner). For an informal bash, kitschy lights in shapes like chili peppers, black spotted cows, pumpkins, and pigs, as well as more traditional Christmas lights or Chinese lanterns, can be strung from trees, rafters, or poles. For more elegant gatherings, choose from a range of sophisticated lighting fixtures intended for garden use. Or you might wish to forego the brighter electric lights for more subtle

oil lamps or candlelight. Flaming torches provide inexpensive and dramatic lighting, but should be placed with consideration to safety. Freestanding open-air fireplaces are also becoming popular, and are functional, too, giving off both light and warmth.

If you plan to use your garden room for entertaining, be sure to include some sort of overhead shelter that offers relief from the blazing sun. A pergola with slatted rafters contributes partial shade while serving as a support for luscious climbers such as trumpet vine or wisteria. Awnings, either permanent or retractable, are also practical

RIGHT: *Bringing indoor furniture outside transforms a poolside snack into a genteel tête-à-tête. Beneath the vine-draped shelter of a pillared roof, a table covered with an antique quilt is surrounded by wooden armchairs. This comfy spot also offers an unparalleled view of turquoise water, stark against the bright, white patio, framed by formal green hedges and earthy terra-cotta containers.*

122

tools for keeping out the elements, though they may not suit every house style. A more temporary and less expensive solution to providing some shelter is to set up several large market umbrellas. These come in a range of sizes, styles, and materials, and can be stored easily when not needed. Another possibility for creating shelter is to site the garden room in the shade of existing trees (but first make sure that the trees are not the kind that drop fruits and seeds all over). You may need to thin the branches of tall trees to admit more light or trim low-hanging branches so guests don't walk into them.

If you plan on having formal events in the garden, consider the type of flooring carefully. Dressy affairs mean high heels, and high heels on cobblestone, gravel, grass, or uneven flagstones could be a recipe for disaster. Quarry tiles and bricks are beautiful, but some become slippery when wet, and some bricks become treacherously moss-covered. Wooden decking, mortared stones such as slate or bluestone, and bricks or concrete pavers should be sufficiently level that even guests who are, shall we say, slightly unsteady on their feet will still be able to negotiate the path and garden room in safety. Decks and patios with stairsteps or multiple levels should be equipped with handrails, and adequate lighting should be provided near any sudden turns or changes in elevation.

123

LEFT: *Luminarias are part of the Spanish/American Indian traditions of the Southwest, but have gained popularity in other areas as well. These inexpensive lights, perfect for adding drama to a nighttime garden party, are created by cuffing paper bags, filling the bottoms with sand or birdseed, and setting long-burning plumber's candles firmly into the sandy bases. This project is well worth the effort for a vision of soft candlelight that, in calm weather, can burn the whole night.*

An outdoor setting should not automatically reduce us to cavemen chowing down around a fire. In fact, it is quite possible to maintain in alfresco dining the same standards observed at the family dinner table (or even higher standards if you are entertaining adults only!). Give the same care and attention to the alfresco table setting that you would to any other dinner party—after all, red-checked oilcloth and paper cups are not the only table decor suitable for the great outdoors. Even a casual get-together can be made more sophisticated if you bring out the "real" table linens and dishes, and more elegant affairs can be made truly special with a magical outdoor setting.

Never underestimate the power of color—if your chairs are bright blue or canary yellow, spotlight that color by repeating it in colorful fabrics on cushions, tablecloths, napkins, and seat covers. Look for tableware and serving pieces that coordinate with your colors, and don't forget to include glassware, flatware with colored handles, pitchers, vases, jardinieres, candles, and even flowers. Also keep an eye out for odd pieces of garden furniture at flea markets and garage sales; these can often be transformed with brightly colored enamel paint.

❧ For a casual affair with a picnic appeal, go for a primary color scheme, with a bright red tablecloth, blue cotton napkins, and lots of chunky candles in assorted sizes (chunky for stability). Bunches of cheery yellow flowers in deep blue glass vases lend an air of grace to the setting. Use everyday stainless steel flatware in a simple pattern and dishes of Fiestaware or stoneware in red, yellow, or blue.

❧ Give an alfresco dinner party with a theme. Be creative, and follow the theme through the table decorations, flowers, music, and food. You might choose something exotic, like a Moroccan casbah setting or a tropical paradise, or perhaps you'd rather try a Western hoedown or an old-fashioned clambake. Let your imagination run wild, considering only what you can accomplish within the limits of your budget and time, and what you think your guests would enjoy.

❧ Revive the tradition of the garden party. An afternoon tea allows plenty of freedom in what you can serve and provides an excellent excuse to bring out all your pretty glassware and silver pieces. Petite sandwiches, little cakes, fresh scones and jam, and, of course, plenty of tea, both hot and iced, let you do most of the work ahead of time so you can enjoy the party.

Mismatched china cups and saucers, beautifully colored Depression-glass plates, and any vintage pieces inherited from grandma are all lovely additions to the tea table. This is the time to bring out your embroidered table linens or lacy cloths. Delicate flowers like tea roses or sweet peas arranged in ceramic teapots or pressed-glass vases complete the scene.

❀ For a special occasion, consider an all-white setting. White against a backdrop of green is a stunning combination, and pale colors are always effective for entertaining after dark, especially when combined with soft lighting that makes them glow.

While some think of white and gold as a winter holiday combination, it is just as elegant and effective on a hot summer evening, when the white cools and the gold glitters in the dark. White tablecloths with woven gold accents, crystal glassware patterned with gold, classic white china edged in gold, a gold-plated candelabra—even gold-plated flatware in ornate designs—can create a luxurious table setting for a memorable occasion.

❀ Late summer or early autumn meals under a harvest moon call for pots of warm-colored chrysanthemums, starry white boltonia, flowering kale, trailing ivy, and ornamental grasses; repeat the theme of autumn flowers and foliage in artful arrangements for the table. Create a seasonal display in the corner of your garden room, deck, or patio with pumpkins, gourds, ornamental corn, and a big scarecrow.

Cover the table with a richly textured cloth—or layers of cloths—in antique gold, spicy pumpkin-orange, deep burgundy, olive green, bronzy browns, or even rich purple.

Use napkins of thick woven cotton in complementary colors or autumnal blends, and set them off with distinctive napkin rings. Heavy amber glassware, tableware in leafy designs or autumnal colors, and an eclectic assortment of pottery serving pieces make the table setting warm and welcoming.

The main thing to remember when decorating an alfresco table is that if it's possible indoors, it can usually be adapted for the outdoors.

BELOW: Even a simple summer lunch of cold salads can be a special event when you bring out china serving plates and decorate the table with the petals of sweet peas and the orange and yellow blooms of nasturtium.

INFORMAL ENTERTAINING

Most families probably use outdoor rooms such as decks and patios for informal gatherings, picnics, and family cookouts more often than any other type of affair. For this type of entertainment, a refined decor is less important that a friendly ambience and a relaxed, comfortable place to sprawl out and dig in, where kids don't have to be on their best behavior and where beverages can unashamedly be served in cans.

This is most likely not the kind of party that you'd invite your boss to attend, but for good friends and neighbors, close family, or your kids' friends, the key words are casual comfort. That is not to say that close friends and family might not enjoy some of the fancy trimmings, too, but you can pick and choose the luxurious extras without worrying too much about serious party etiquette. Younger children like nothing better than a picnic, and for them, the food hardly matters—watermelon and other messy fruits, peanut butter and jelly, pizza, salad and vegetables picked fresh from the garden, all are delightful when eaten outdoors, far from the daily rigors of table manners. Have the kids wear swimming suits to the picnic and just hose them down afterwards.

For a family barbecue, keep the grill a safe distance from the kids and the house, but close enough to a doorway that food can be ferried from kitchen to grill without too much interference. If the grill is likely to produce a lot of smoke, make sure the table and chairs are upwind from the cooking area. Have plenty of "weights" on hand to anchor tablecloths, napkins, and other accessories that might be carried off by a brisk breeze. Special tablecloth weights that fasten to the cloth's corners are available, while beautiful, smooth stones add perfect heft to tablethings.

While bugs can ruin an outdoor gathering, particularly at night, think twice before installing a bug-zapper—not only is the sound of electrocution extremely unappetizing, scientists have also confirmed that the "zapping" explodes the insects' bodies and sprays minuscule bug parts and bacteria into the air around the zapper. Softer lighting is less likely to attract bugs and is also much more conducive to relaxation and conversation. Try traditional candles, torches, or tiny tealights.

A picnic or barbecue does not necessarily mean plastic tablecloths and paper plates; there is no reason that an informal table should not also be attractive and appealing. Everyday stoneware or brightly colored tableware can be used to dress up a casual

127

OPPOSITE: *An informal meal such as breakfast is perfect for enjoying out of doors. Instead of transporting entrees and lots of side dishes outside and worrying about keeping them at the proper temperature, you can simply set out fruit, croissants and bagels, and juice or coffee. This type of casual meal allows you to focus instead on the pretty extras, like this colorful tablecloth accented with geranium-filled terra-cotta pots, and gives you plenty of time for chatting with your guests.*

If you like a casual, thrown-together affair, be glad that you do not live in Victorian times, when picnics were quite a chore, according to Mrs. Beeton in her famous cookery book (Mrs. Beeton's Cookery Book, New and Enlarged Edition, Ward, Lock, Bowden & Co., London, 1891).

A more troublesome luncheon to provide is one for a picnic. We do not mean one of those grand ones where the same viands as would be found at an invitation lunch in a large establishment would be served with the same state and ceremony; but a delightfully informal meal perhaps got together at a day's notice where the different members of the party each make some contribution to the feast.

Now for this kind of meal it is not only essential that we have a menu, we also need a complete list of all articles required, independent of the actual food and drink.

Mrs. Beeton suggests that a picnic luncheon for twelve people should include sardine sandwiches, one large pigeon pie, six pounds of cold beef, horse-radish sauce, cucumber salad and dressing, fruit or jam puffs, two moulds of blancmange, one pound of cheese biscuits, two quarts of strawberries, two pounds of cherries, three loaves of bread, and half a pound of butter. Which they'd have to eat pretty quickly in order to be ready for tea. Which would hopefully be just enough to tide them over until dinner—of six courses or more.

ABOVE: *You needn't go to the trouble of a proper Victorian lunch—call your two best friends, bring out your finest silver, china, and table linens, and enjoy the pretty setting and good company.*

place setting, accented with a pretty tablecloth and fabric napkins if the hostess feels so inclined. If you'd rather use disposable plates and cups to prevent breakage and cut down on cleanup, spring for the heavy chinette, which comes in attractive patterns and colors. Flatware can be dressy or casual, although plastic pieces are sometimes necessary when there isn't enough of the good forks and knives to go around or if you want to simply throw everything away at the end of the picnic. Even if you elect to use disposable tableware, bring out some good serving pieces and serve the food from platters and bowls that will please the eye. Some of the most artful table arrangements combine casual items with elegant accents—decorate the table with bowls of fruits or pitchers filled with freshly picked flowers, and make a welcoming oasis with lush arrangements of hanging baskets and containers.

Although it is tempting to leave the food outside so people can continue to munch, it's healthier from a food safety standpoint if you clear the table right after eating (and you're less likely to attract insects). The quickest way to do this is to put the kids to work, but if your helpers vanish, other alternatives include wheeled carts and large trays. If you have a kitchen window overlooking the eating area and closer than the door, set up a relay and pass things through the windows to someone inside. Do cover the food and get it refrigerated, but don't do the dishes right away unless you can turn it into a social event. No matter how perfect the food, the flowers, and the ambience, the host and/or hostess must be able to relax and enjoy themselves, too!

LEFT: *A breezy orchard is the perfect spot for a casual alfresco meal with family and friends. The rustic table and folding chairs and blue-checked tablecloth announce simple picnic fare; the fresh-mowed lawn ensures plenty of space for romping children.*

Fruits used to be grown in orchards and vegetables were set in long, neatly hoed rows, while herbs were confined to herb gardens. These sections of the garden were considered necessary, but nothing to brag about. They were tucked into a side corner of the yard, close to the kitchen to make harvesting easy, and often separated from the "ornamental" part of the garden by a brick wall or tall hedge. While today's kitchen gardens may still be walled or separated from the "main" garden, they are usually treated as one of the most useful garden rooms, and are often among the most ornamental. While a serviceable garden of the past might have been stocked with staples such as lettuce and tomatoes, carrots and runner beans, squashes and sprouts, today's gardens are likely to include many exotic fruits and vegetables, fresh herbs, and colorful cultivars that can hold their own in a flower border.

A modern kitchen garden often borrows from the best British and European traditions, Mediterranean-style herb gardens, French potagers, German four-square plots, and fenced or walled British kitchen gardens, as well as the standard American gardens with long rows to hoe. The kitchen garden today may be as compact as a couple of containers on a balcony or rooftop or as large as a rural gardener's side pasture. Many kitchen gardens are designed to support a home-based industry—homemade jams and jellies, salsas and pasta sauces, or herbal vinegars and salad dressings. Other gardeners just want their kitchen garden to supply

fresh fruits and vegetables for the family dinner and herbs for the pot. Whatever the style and size of a kitchen garden, it effectively becomes a garden room that is integral to both the exterior design and interior function of the home.

*Combining form and function, kitchen gardens may be accented with arbors, trellises, or tall stakes bound into "teepees" and covered with vining plants such as scarlet runner beans (*Phaseolus coccineus*), small ornamental gourds, golden hop vines (*Humulus lupulus 'Aureus'*), grape vines (*Vitis spp.*), or purple hyacinth beans (*Dolichos lablab*), as well as some vines grown primarily for their flowers, such as morning glory (*Ipomoea spp.*), nasturtium (*Tropaeolum majus*), and cardinal vine (*Ipomocea quamoclit*). Good edging plants for knot gardens, raised beds, or four-square gardens include boxwood (*Buxus spp.*), lavender (*Lavandula spp.*), rosemary (*Rosmarinus spp.*)—in regions with very mild winters—ornamental kale (*Brassica oleracea*), alpine strawberries (*Fragraria alpina, syn. F. vesca 'Semperflorens'*), chives (*Allium schoenoprasum*), silver-mound artemisia (*Artemisia schmidtiana 'Silver Mound'*), neat mounds of globe basil (*Ocimum spp.*) or the interesting Thai basil (*Ocimum basilicum 'Siam Queen'*), thyme (*Thymus spp.*), blue fescue (*Festuca ovina var. glauca*), lavender cotton (*Santolina chamaecyparissus*), globe amaranth (*Gomphrena globosa*), or small marigolds (*Tagetes spp.*). To cut down on maintenance and to make weeding*

130

and harvesting easier, kitchen gardens usually have well-defined paths or hardscaped borders that prevent plants from wandering out of bounds. Raised beds and large containers make plants accessible, though regular watering and fertilization are essential for potted plants, and the soil may need to be replaced or refreshed periodically as well.

Mixing annuals, as well as some biennials and perennials, into kitchen gardens for added color is an accepted practice in both modern and traditional kitchen gardens. Only recently, though, have fruits and vegetables become ornamental enough to be included in perennial beds and borders. This practice can add a whole new dimension to the design of the garden, but note that for the best productivity many fruits and vegetables need less competition than they'll get in a flower bed.

If you are one of those gardeners who has never tried growing a kitchen garden, experimenting with blueberry bushes, tiny alpine strawberries, dramatic rhubarb, brilliant Swiss chard, and even 'Malabar' spinach may be all the inspiration you need to discover these plots of culinary delight. Those who look for fragrance won't be able to resist planting a variety of scented marigolds and containers of assorted mints, as well as thyme, marjoram, oregano, lemon balm, and the many forms of basil that look great, taste good, and, when you rub your fingers on the leaves, smell heavenly.

If, on the other hand, you have been growing edible plants for so long that the whole discussion of kitchen gardens seems ho-hum, try planting a few heirloom varieties. These may be more challenging to grow, because many lack the disease resistance, heat and drought tolerance, and other improvements made by modern breeders, but their unusual appearances, forms, and tastes may well spark new interest in edible plants. Form fanatics should check out angelica, artichokes, and the related cardoons, while those who crave color will be intrigued by 'Ruby Red' and 'Bright Yellow' Swiss chard, 'Neon' eggplants, 'Violet Queen' cauliflower, 'Osaka Purple' mustard green, 'Islander' sweet peppers, and 'Pretty in Purple' hot peppers. Who ever thought browsing a catalog of vegetable seeds could be stimulating to so many senses? No wonder the kitchen garden is one of the most useful, attractive, and potentially exciting of all outdoor rooms.

ABOVE: Vegetables, fruits, and herbs can be every bit as ornamental as flowers, if somewhat more subtle in their charms. Consider the cream-streaked purple of this glossy 'Rosa Bianca' eggplant.

131

While garden rooms are extensions of interior living areas, they face practicalities that don't arise in indoor spaces. For instance, living room furniture needn't be weatherproof, but outdoor pieces certainly must stand up to the elements. Outdoor furniture that will reside in a somewhat protected area, such a porch or a gazebo, may be less weather-resistant than those pieces that will sit out in the garden or on an open patio, but all must be suitable for exterior use. Ideally, all garden furniture should be stored indoors in the winter to extend its life, but this may not be practical if your space is limited. Inexpensive wood, plastic, wicker, rattan, and furniture with glass or canvas accents should definitely be brought indoors for the winter. Cast-iron and other cast-metal furniture can be left outside but it may need rust-proofing and regular painting with weather-resistant paint. Check the manufacturer's instructions and follow their recommendations for weather-proofing your furniture.

Wicker is a classic material for garden rooms, and is perhaps most appropriate for a porch or another sheltered spot, since it should not be exposed to harsh weather. Wicker furniture is woven with rattan, reeds, willow, cane, or synthetic fibers, and its durability and resistance to moisture depend on which material is used. Traditional organic materials have the most charm, but if your family is hard on furniture or if you want it to last, one of the new synthetics may be your best bet. Settees, chairs, hassocks, and tables are all available in vintage or new wicker, and can be had in an array of styles, from simple to elaborate.

Wicker furniture, and indeed wood and metal pieces too, are often outfitted with cushions. In a sheltered spot, or if you plan to put the cushions out only when needed, you may wish to use cotton fabric. If your garden room is exposed to the elements, one of the new synthetic fibers is probably more practical. Acrylics and vinyl-coated polyesters are designed to resist dirt and mildew and to keep their colors even after several seasons in the sun. Of course, if you live in a particularly humid or rainy climate, you will probably need to replace cushions and pillows more often, as constant moisture takes a toll even on relatively weather-resistant fabrics.

Wood furniture may be a good choice if your garden room will be sited out in the open. Teak is a beautiful, long-lasting wood that is extremely well-suited for outdoor use; unfortunately, wood of such quality comes at a rather high cost. Less expensive wood

132

OPPOSITE: *A cast-metal café table and a couple of folding garden chairs are attractive, inexpensive, and can be easily moved and stored indoors for the winter (many such café tables have removable tops so that the table can be stored efficiently). Even simple chairs can be dressed up with comfy cushions, while a table constructed on simple lines can be made more dramatic with a bold display of flowers or an interesting container.*

134

furniture may need regular coating with water-resistant paint, stain, or varnish to prevent the wood from succumbing to mildew and rot. Teak furniture tends to come in simple, timeless designs, although more formal or intricate designs are available at a price. Rustic wooden furniture constructed out of timbers and twigs is extremely decorative and unusual, but not always sturdy or comfortable, so select pieces of this style with care.

Cast iron is also a good option for garden room furniture, but like wood, it must be treated regularly to prevent rust. Many antique and reproduction pieces are available today, though they do tend to be expensive. Iron's weight is desirable if you plan to leave your pieces in one place, but if you need a flexible space where furniture must constantly be moved, it is probably not the material for you. Other metals, such as cast-aluminum or heavy-gauge steel, are more portable, and are relatively maintenance-free. Wirework furniture, which first became popular in the Victorian era and is enjoying a resurgence today, is also lightweight, but may be on the delicate side for family use.

Perhaps the most versatile and common piece of garden furniture is the bench. Often made of wood or wood in combination with metal, a bench can be placed to invite silent contemplation of the garden, or may be situated for convivial chats with friends. A popular convention in medieval times was the exedra, a semicircular seat designed to encourage conversation. This type of conversational seating is often found in sunken gardens or on stone or brick patios sited a step or two below ground level, a position that lends an air of privacy to the space. If you have a retaining wall or are planning to build one, a bench can easily be built into the wall, providing visual interest to the solid wall and a secluded seat for a tête-à-tête.

Another type of traditional bench is built to encircle the trunk of a large, old shade tree. This type of seating is very attractive, and is available with or without backs. Semicircular sections of wrought iron that fit together around the tree are sometimes used to create these seats, and a few modular, prefabricated wooden kits for such benches are now available. Predictably, the nicest of the tree seats are made to order by craftsmen in wood, and they do not come cheap, but may be a worthwhile investment if you love the look.

Traditional garden benches in British, European, and American designs abound in garden catalogs and at garden retailers (see Resources). Consider a classic green Monet-style bench or the spare simplicity of a Mission-style piece. Beautiful and functional benches in myriad styles and materials are widely available—all you need to do is choose one that fits the style of your garden and your life.

Hammocks are the ultimate symbol of sedentary summer: when the lawn is mowed and the weeding done, it's time to settle into the hammock with a frosted glass of lemonade nearby and a Miss Marple mystery ready to prop on your stomach. Well, even if that never happens, it's nice to know that the hammock is ready and waiting. In the olden days, a hammock required two sturdy shade trees with branches at just the right height. Then someone invented the hammock frame, a metal structure that comes apart for easier storage and makes it possible to relocate the hammock into the shade, near the babbling brook, under the lilacs, or anywhere else you may want it. On the other hand, it's not really so lightweight that you'd want to be relocating the hammock every five minutes. While comic strip artists love to show weary (or just lazy) homeowners basking in their hammocks, in truth it's mainly kids I've seen in hammocks, and then they were usually trying to spin it around and flip themselves out. But you really do need a hammock for those lazy days that are always just around the corner. Trust me.

BELOW: A simple Adirondack-style double-seater has been allowed to weather to a lovely silvery gray. Set in the midst of a cottage garden in full bloom, the bench is situated to take full advantage of the glorious fragrances, sights, and sounds of summer.

135

If garden rooms bring the indoors out, then solariums, screened-in porches, and the like bring the outdoors in—almost. Solariums (rooms with strong exposure to sunlight, often with a glass ceiling and at least two walls of mostly glass) let in the sun without exposing plants to seasonal extremes, while screened-in porches do the same with one difference—they offer protection from the hot sun. The most practical screened-in porches have screened panels that can be easily switched for glass panes in winter. These rooms are betwixt and between, halfway outdoors and halfway in, and they combine the pleasures of a greenhouse with the comfort of a living room. They also offer decorative opportunities that are not possible in greenhouses or living rooms.

Before deciding whether to add a solarium or screened-in porch to your home, note that each has its particular virtues, and these attributes may make one of the rooms more suitable for certain uses or regions than the other. In hot, humid climates, for instance, a screened-in porch is much desired because it lets in breezes while keeping out the hottest rays of sun. In dry, desertlike areas, a solarium offers bright sunlight while protecting tender plants from the sudden drop in evening temperatures. Solariums also enable plant lovers in cold-winter regions to stretch the season by bringing plants indoors and exposing them to every stingy ray of winter sun. Screened-in porches allow for the pleasures of outdoor entertaining without subjecting guests to the predictable bugs and unpredictable weather.

Protected structures such as solariums and screened-in porches offer gardeners an opportunity to try growing exotic tropicals or lush houseplants. These plants can be moved outdoors when the weather is hot and damp (tropicals don't usually like dry heat), and moved back inside when it is windy, cold, or otherwise inhospitable. As with all container plants, it is important to provide a suitable growing medium, fertilizer when needed, and pots with sufficient drainage and of an appropriate size—they should be large enough that the plants will not become rootbound or top heavy. Solariums may provide sufficient light in late winter or early spring for starting trays of seeds indoors, while screened-in porches are perfect for hardening off seeds that have sprouted and are ready for transplanting.

Solariums and screened-in porches are often used as links from the deck, patio, or garden to the main house, offering a smooth transition between outdoor and indoor living spaces. The furniture often reflects the room's transitional role—the pieces are perhaps more formal than those on the deck or in the garden, but still have a "garden" aesthetic. Simple wicker outfitted with luxurious cushions is an excellent choice, as are wrought-iron café tables and chairs. Sculptures and decorative accents can help emphasize the sense of the room as an indoor garden, while elegant fabrics create a luxurious ambience that would be impractical on a deck exposed to all seasons.

If your house already features a solarium or screened-in porch, consider yourself fortunate and make the most of this useful space. If you are dreaming of additions to your house and garden, these are beautifully practical rooms to consider.

BELOW: *A sun-filled solarium or screened-in porch may be the best alternative to an outdoor room for those who live in climates that give outdoor living a short shrift. Robust container plantings can contribute to the feel of an outdoor garden setting, and the weatherproof interior allows greater latitude when it comes to selecting furniture and fabrics.*

137

Chapter Six

SERENE SPACES

A ROOM OF ONE'S OWN

PAGES 138-139: *A cozy seating area in a sheltered spot and a fringed hammock swinging in the dappled shade of tall trees gives this garden room a tranquil ambience. Many people plan their outdoor spaces with a focus on entertaining, forgetting to set aside a spot for rest and relaxation. A shady corner is the perfect place for such a retreat, where cooling breezes rustle the leaves and the loudest noise is the busy chattering of birds.*

140

OPPOSITE: *A small walled garden may be all the green space required. This city garden, just off a townhouse living room, is an instant getaway. Landscaped entirely with container plants, the plant palette is made up mainly of soothing foliage punctuated by airy white flowers.*

While the first outdoor living spaces or garden rooms that we create tend to be adapted for activities such as cooking and entertaining, it is also important to design a space that is soothing to the soul. This garden room acts as a refuge—not simply a place to relax, but a sanctuary reserved for meditation and renewal of inner resources. The twenty-first century promises to be faster-paced and busier than any era of the past, and it is easy to become overwhelmed by the need for multitasking and the minute-by-minute scheduling that has become a fact of modern life. Today, we are beginning to recognize the importance of building in time and places for serenity in a world where chaos and confusion are as much a part of our lives as the air we breathe.

The best part of a garden designed as a refuge is that it is a supremely personal space, where the colors, textures, shapes, and sounds that please the creator can have free rein. Especially common in serene spaces are water features. Flowing water contributes a sense of both calm and energy, along with the comforting idea that the world is constantly renewing itself. Still water is peaceful and quite literally reflective, inspiring contemplation in those who view it.

A serene garden room may be enhanced by high, vine-covered walls that hide it from the rest of the world, though this is certainly not a requirement. The elements of the garden should consist of plants and features that are restful to you; they should create a peaceful vista and a sense of oneness with nature. The details may vary, but certain elements of a peaceful garden seem to strike a chord in many of us.

❂ A comfortable place to sit. Kids may be comfortable flopped down on their stomachs in the grass, but as we get older a bench holds more appeal than the hard ground.

Consider both aesthetics and comfort—a stone bench may look wonderful in a leafy glen, but it could become very hard and cold if you plan on sitting for any length of time. A teak bench contoured for comfort and sturdy enough to withstand time and weather could well be worth the initial expense. A cozy garden swing encourages peaceful contemplation.

⊘ Something to focus on. It's fine to have a comfortable place to sit, but if you don't have something restful to focus on, you will soon become bored and fidgety. Or you may just fall asleep. Naps are good, but it's also necessary to give your waking mind a vacation—sitting still and absorbing the sights and sounds of the garden is an easy and practical solution to information overload. Focus on a sundial, a birdbath, or a large urn placed at the end of a vista directly in line with your bench, or put a unique garden

RIGHT: *A corner of a patio has been converted into a charming hideaway. The level change (note the step up), wall of colored glass, and bowerlike arrangement of plants define this as a place apart. At once sunny and shady, the room is both comfortable and comforting—a delightful spot to gather your thoughts, pot up a few plants, or catch up on correspondence.*

142

sculpture in the place of honor. Set the bench in front of a serene water pond, a fragrant herb garden, or beneath an arbor of sweetly scented, old-fashioned roses; try 'Zephirine Drouhin' or White Lady Banks rose. Center your thoughts on the view ahead and set your mind free.

⊘ Life is in the details. How easy it is to overlook the butterflies, hummingbirds, and even the pretty moths as we rush to and from our cars. How easy it is to miss the bird-calls and the summer sounds of tree frogs, buzzing bees, and softly tinkling wind chimes. Plant your garden refuge to invite visits from birds, butterflies, intriguing insects, and other forms of wildlife (fruiting shrubs and native species of flowers are your best bets). For the time being, forget that the rabbits are eating your perennials, the deer are feeding on your hostas, and the moles are making a mess of it all. Revel in your connection with the land, the plants, and all the life forms that surround you. Remind yourself that there is more to civilization than blacktop roads and air-conditioned rooms.

⊘ A garden for all the senses. Make your garden a treat for all five senses—include beautiful and restful vistas; plants and garden accents with different textures to stimulate the sense of touch; tinkling water or wind chimes to soothe the ears; and plenty of fragrant flowers or foliage to excite the sense of smell.

⊘ A secret space. A garden refuge need not be completely closed off or hidden away, but an element of privacy, an indication that this particular garden room is a serene and secret space, should somehow be conveyed. Perhaps the garden can be partially walled or fenced, leaving an open area for a vista, or you may wish to separate the room with a dense hedge that acts as a screen. A tall, shady tree not only provides protection from the hot sun, but creates a leafy ceiling that emphasizes the sense of enclosure.

⊘ A place for spiritual renewal. Each of us needs to open ourselves to something greater than we are in order to preserve our humility and our humanity. It is all too easy to become mechanized in dealing with people, even with those closest to us, when we lose control of our lives. Rebuild your sense of self and your connection with the spiritual and natural world by devoting a small part of your day or week to spiritual renewal. "Burnout" is more than a buzzword, it is a fact of life that does untold damage to individuals and families, and gardens are great places to let healing begin. Creating a garden is a lot of work, and the more I garden the more I realize that not everything is within my control.

BELOW: *The pedestal supporting this statue is almost as artistic as the piece on display. Combined, the statue and its support are like a visual magnet, drawing the eye unerringly to the face that looks as if it was copied from a Roman coin. Note how the surrounding foliage highlights the statue instead of hiding it.*

143

The concept of a moon garden may have originated in the days when farmers planted certain crops during particular phases of the moon. It was believed that the moon's gravitational pull could influence growth. Therefore, it was believed that the best time to plant seedlings was during the moon's third quarter, on the assumption that when the moon is on the wane, leaf growth slows down and root growth increases.

Today, moon gardens often have more prosaic rationales. Many people spend most of their days at work, and have time to enjoy their gardens primarily in the evenings. A garden that comes to life when the sun goes down fits perfectly into the lifestyle of working people.

Moon gardens, sometimes called evening gardens, don't have to be elaborate; in fact, they are often most effective when experienced in a more intimate way. To create a moon garden, first select a good spot for a bench, a cozy grouping of chairs, or even a garden swing. If you have a pond or other water feature, arrange the seating where you can overlook the water and view the soothing reflections of moon and trees across the water's surface. Landscape lighting is an essential element of a moon garden—sometimes even the moon can use a little help. Soft, diffuse lighting is best, created by unobtrusive lighting fixtures placed where visitors to the garden will not trip over them.

Plants for moon gardens are primarily white, because white reflects light and appears to shine in the darkness, although some pastel-colored flowers also seem to glow brightly at night. Since many flowers' fragrance becomes more pronounced at night—flowering tobacco, lilies, tuberose—the moon garden is usually filled with delicate perfume. In addition, there are many flowers that keep their blossoms tightly furled during the day and only open at night. Be sure to include a few flowers of this type in any moon garden—try 'Moon Frolic' or 'Butterpat' daylilies or a night-blooming evening primrose (Oenothera spp.). Bear in mind that a moon garden can be as large or small as you like—it may simply be a grouping of plant-filled pots set in a crescent shape around a table and chairs, accompanied by soft lighting and the ethereal tinkling of wind chimes. Or you might like to create a larger-scale garden room designed for evening, with a full complement of white blossoms and night-blooming plants. A well-designed moon garden should look as good during the day as it does at night, but luckily most plants ideal for moon gardens are attractive in sunlit hours, too. Following is a selected list of good plants for a moon garden. Choose white-flowering or pastel varieties of plants that come in an array of colors:

Anemones (Anemone × hybrida)
Angel's trumpet (Datura inoxia)
Artemisia (Artemisia *spp.*)
Carnations (Dianthus *spp.*)
Evening primrose (Oenothera *spp.*)

144

*Feverfew (*Matricaria capensis*)*
*Flowering tobacco (*Nicotiana *spp.)*
*Garden Queen Anne's lace (*Ammi majus*)*
*Honeysuckle (*Lonicera *spp.)*
*Judd viburnum (*Viburnum juddii*)*
*Koreanspice viburnum (*Viburnum carlesii*)*
*Lilacs (*Syringa *spp.)*
*Lilies (*Lilium *spp.)*
*Lily-of-the-valley (*Convallaria majalis*)*
*Magnolias (*Magnolia *spp.)*
*Mock orange (*Philadelphus *spp.),*
*Moonflower (*Ipomoea alba*)*

*Narcissus (*Narcissus *spp.)*
*Rhododendrons (*Rhododendron *spp.)*
*Roses (*Rosa *spp.)*
*Spider flower (*Cleome hasslerana*)*
*Sweet alyssum (*Lobularia maritima*)*
*Water lilies (*Nymphaea *spp.)*
*White coneflower (*Echinacea purpurea*
    'Alba' or 'White Swan')*
*White-variegated hostas (*Hosta *spp.)*

BELOW: The pure white blossoms of profusely blooming 'Honorine Jobert' anemones demonstrate the beauty of white flowers in an evening garden, reflecting the moonlight and brightening the torchlit surroundings.

145

JAPANESE INFLUENCES:
SIMPLE AND SERENE

While relatively few North Americans have had the opportunity to visit Japan's famous gardens in person, just about anyone interested in gardening has a mental image of at least some of the elements found in Japanese gardens. We see green oases with exquisite landscape trees pruned in an open-branched style; we see rocks and pebbles used in dynamic ways; we see gently flowing water.

A garden in the Japanese style generally includes a water feature such as a pond or waterfall, although water may also be represented symbolically by a riverbed of smooth stones, pebbles, or sand. Small rocks and large stones also play a part in the traditional Japanese garden, as focal points and as important features in the re-creation of natural scenes. Bridges, shrines, statuary, and structures with strong architectural features may also figure prominently in many Japanese-style gardens, although some take the minimalist line and reduce the landscape to only a few essential elements. "Borrowed" vistas and man-made vistas are often important aspects of the Japanese garden, and are used to frame distant mountains or focus on a particular feature.

Dry gardens may include a floor pattern made up of smooth stones in a similar color and texture, with an "ocean" of carefully raked gravel highlighted by "islands" of stones or moss. Some minimalist gardens include only one or two plants, relying on hardscape materials to convey the spirit of the garden. More traditional Japanese gardens include plant materials such as moss, bamboo (*Arundinaria* spp., *Pleiblastus* spp., *Sasa* spp., etc.), azaleas (*Rhododendron* spp.), rhododendrons (*Rhododendron* spp.), camellias (*Camellia* spp.), wisteria (*Wisteria* spp.), flowering quince (*Chaenomeles speciosa*), cherry and plum (both *Prunus* spp.), a few perennials such as peonies (*Paeonia* spp.) and irises (*Iris* spp.), artistically pruned pines (*Pinus* spp.), *Cryptomeria* and other conifers, shade trees such as ginkgo (*Ginkgo* spp.) and maple (*Acer* spp.), old-fashioned spireas (*Spiraea* spp.), and countless forms of Japanese maple (*Acer palmatum*, *A. japonica*).

When considering a Japanese-style garden room, bear in mind that while these gardens have the appearance of simplicity, in fact they may be a challenge to maintain, especially if you have dogs, cats, or children who will be tempted to run through the

OPPOSITE: *A Japanese lantern at the edge of a pond creates a fitting spot to stop and reflect. Rich in texture and subtle color, this garden is visually exciting, yet retains its tranquil air.*

carefully raked oceans of gravel. If you have a family that uses your garden room vigorously, some of the more delicate elements of a Japanese garden may be inappropriate. Instead, you might choose to incorporate plants that are representative of the Japanese style, with small water features and a few sculptures or garden ornaments.

Unless you are a purist, you can always combine elements from Japanese gardens with structures and ornaments that have meaning to you to create a space suitable for meditation or prayer. Include soothing sounds of water in a fountain, or soft wind chimes or tinkling bells, as well as subtle landscape lighting to create a restful mood near a bench or gazebo. Be sure to include places in the garden where you can sit and enjoy the view, the quickest way to find serenity in what may be a deceptively simple garden design.

OPPOSITE: *The still water creates a silvery surface, reflecting plants and sky as in a photographic negative. Low mounds of trees act in counterpoint to the small, round leaves of the water lilies. Form and foliage, light and shadow are the essence of this design.*

BELOW: *Azalea blossoms cascade around a small statue, posing pensively at the waterside. Flowering shrubs, perhaps as much as any other feature, create the impression of a Japanese-style garden.*

Bonsai, Penjing, and Topiary

However much we talk about "natural gardening," the act of gardening itself is unnatural: we level the ground, remove weeds, put the plants we select where we want them to grow, and hybridize them to produce the color, size, and form that we desire. The fact that we frequently succeed only indicates that we have serendipitously managed to put the plants where they were supposed to be! With bonsai, penjing, and topiary, we gardeners have taken another step closer to controlling nature by encouraging, or sometimes forcing, plants to grow into a desired shape or miniaturized form. There is a certain amount of confusion about these three art forms, which are basically different methods of pruning and training plants into stylized forms. They share a common benefit in that all three may be performed indoors with containerized plants, instead of only outside in the garden.

BONSAI

Although some sources describe bonsai as being developed in the Orient almost two thousand years ago, it is generally believed that the Japanese art of bonsai evolved much more recently out of the far more ancient Chinese penjing. Cultural exchanges between China and Japan in the twelfth century introduced Zen Buddhism, with its emphasis on enlightenment, to Japan (it was known as Ch'an Buddhism in China). Historical records suggest that the Japanese practice of bonsai began about this same time. Like penjing,

bonsai is an art based on contemplative, inspirational, even spiritual themes.

Bonsai refers to trees in shallow containers that have been thinned, pruned, clipped, and wired into artistically stylized and aesthetically pleasing miniature trees. (Note that full-sized trees that have been similarly pruned and trained are not considered bonsai.) As with penjing, the appearance of great age is a desired result, and, in fact, many trees trained in this fashion do live to a significant age.

As with any container plant, bonsai, penjing, and potted topiary plants are dependent on the gardener to provide adequate water, air, sunlight, and fertilizer as needed, as well as protection from insects, diseases, and extremes of weather. The appropriate temperature and amount of light will depend in part on the plant material used. There is an abundance of written material available on this subject, as well as a number of bonsai clubs with websites and links on the internet (see Resources).

PENJING

Although penjing is not very well known in North America, this Chinese art is believed to predate bonsai significantly. Penjing can be traced back to China's T'ang Dynasty (618–907), when it was recorded in paintings of the period, and enjoyed continued popularity through the twentieth

150

century. There are many similarities between penjing, which literally means "scenery in a pot or container," and bonsai, which means "tree in a shallow container or pot." H. Marc Cathey, former director of the U.S. National Arboretum, in an article in American Horticulturist, describes Chinese penjing as related to temperate and tropical species planted in natural clays trained into a form that is ascending and which emphasizes the trunk and root. In comparison, he explains Japanese bonsai as involving mostly hardy native trees and shrubs trained into a form that is "dimensional" and has depth and lushness with the foliage emphasized.

BELOW: Carefully prepared planting mixtures, precise pruning techniques, and a sense of the plants potential shape and appearance are all elements of bonsai planting techniques. Conifers as well as deciduous trees, flowering plants, and plants with delicate foliage can all be trained into bonsai form.

Penjing is traditionally divided into three categories:

◉ *Tree Penjing (shumu penjing)—similar to bonsai; involves creating a well-proportioned, miniature tree in a container, giving the impression that the tree is of a great age.*

◉ *Landscape Penjing (shanshui penjing)—rocks, instead of trees, are the focus of this form of penjing, which is intended to create the impression of panoramic mountain views. Chinese rocks often used in these formations are called Turtle-Shell rock and Yin Tak rock.*

◉ *Water-and-Land Penjing (shuihan penjing)—a combination of rocks, trees, and water used to replicate the elements of a natural landscape in miniature form. Common themes include island, creek, river, or lake, or a combination of features.*

The goal of penjing is to re-create a scene from nature in a container—the scene should exist not just as an artistic endeavor but should also express the essence and spirit of the original landscape. Balance and harmony and the interplay of opposites—is an important element of penjing, as is a sense of movement and interconnectedness.

TOPIARY

Topiary, opus toparium *in the original Latin, is the "Edward Scissorhands" school of pruning. It is an ancient art described by Pliny the Elder in the first century A.D.; Pliny credited the invention of topiary to a contemporary of Julius Caesar more than one hundred years earlier. The art form enjoyed a resurgence of popularity during the Italian Renaissance, when knot gardens and shrubs cut into exotic or animal shapes became all the rage. The Dutch, the English, and the French enthusiastically adopted topiary, though each tradition had its distinctive stylistic differences. The interest in topiary waxed and waned throughout the nineteenth and twentieth centuries, gaining in popularity toward the end of each century. Topiary can be found in both public and private gardens today, as well as in the gardens of commercial buildings and tourist spots like Florida's Disney World.*

Topiary may be created on a hollow form stuffed with Styrofoam, sterile soilless growing media, and spaghnum moss, or may be assembled using variations of the above materials, for instance plants like ivy may be trained over a chicken wire frame or "plugged" into a form. Topiary shapes can also be carved into existing, densely branched shrubs such as boxwood (Buxus spp.) or yew (Taxus spp.). An endless variety of animals and other whimsical shapes can be created with topiary—virtually any design your imagination can conceive can be executed, with limitations set only by the designer's skill.

OPPOSITE: *In addition to bonsai, penjing, and topiary, the pruning of full-sized trees may be raised to an art. The judicious pruning of this Japanese maple, as demonstrated so vividly against the background of brilliant autumn color, emphasizes the drama of the tree's form.*

152

T he practice of *feng shui* (literally "wind-water") can be traced back to the T'ang Dynasty in China, with roots that are believed to be based on the *I-Ching*, or *Book of Changes*. One of the best known feng shui masters was Yang Yun-Sang, who served as an advisor in the court of T'ang Emperor Hi Tsang in the ninth century A.D. Most of the feng shui concepts used today are based on principles recorded in several texts compiled by Yang.

In recent years, Westerners have become enchanted by the philosophies of feng shui, and consultants and books of advice abound. Without going into great detail about this complex subject, we'll explore a few theories that are integral to its practice. One of the most important principles to understand is the Trinity of Luck, which consists of Heaven Luck, or, roughly speaking, destiny; Man Luck, or that which a person achieves through his or her own efforts; and Earth Luck, or the luck that can be influenced through the practice of feng shui. Practitioners believe that peace and prosperity can be gained by learning how to live in harmony with nature and with one's surroundings. Energy or life forces, called *ch'i*, are described as similar to radio waves, and these impulses are classified symbolically with reference to a celestial dragon.

Feng shui theories can be broken down into the Form School, which focuses on the home and environment, and the Compass School, which is composed of the Eight Mansions School, aimed at determining a person's prime energy direction to identify "directions" in a person's life that could have a positive or a negative influence. The Flying Stars School, the second aspect of the Compass School, is based on a theory of time as well as productive and destructive elements connected to the five elements of fire, water, wood, metal, and the earth. Symbols for fire include the color red, the direction south, and the season summer. Water is symbolically represented by the color black, the direction north, and the season winter. Wood represents the east as well as the color green; metal symbolizes the west as well as the colors white and sometimes gold. Earth is represented by the color yellow and is the directional center.

The methods and practices of the different schools of feng shui are quite complicated, but with regard to a landscape, there are a few basic guidelines. Wind, for instance, is believed to be the "breath of the green dragon" or the "cosmic ch'i." Wind can blow the good luck away, and fast-flowing water can also carry ch'i away. Therefore,

154

landscapes sheltered from the wind, and with slow-moving (but not still) water features, are considered to be landscapes where ch'i can accumulate and therefore do good. It is also believed that the symbolic green dragon and white tiger can be found in natural formations such as hills, mountains, and rivers, but that their presence can be determined only by following clues hidden in the natural contours and elevation of the land, the direction of water flow, and the type and color of vegetation and soil.

Because the principles of feng shui must to be applied to each garden specifically, it is difficult to generalize methods of enhancing ch'i. Feng shui consultants often design gardens that not only stress balance and energy, but also center on specific themes. A feng shui garden may be designed as a meditation garden, a healing garden, or even as a garden that brings power to the gardener. Depending on the goal of the design, different principles apply. A few general principles do pertain to almost any feng shui garden, however:

⊘ Balance is extremely important; consider not only the balance of proportion, but also the balance of elements such as light and shade.

LEFT: *Many elements work together in creating a garden that follows the principles of feng shui. Running water, here expressed with a fountain issuing from a rock and traveling to a pool, is a common theme. In the absence of a stream, water is often represented by stone waterfalls or stone-filled dry streambeds. Curved lines, hills and valleys, and other landscape formations are used to direct the flow of energy known as ch'i.*

Ch'i, or energy, must be able to flow in a free, relaxed manner through the garden. To encourage this, incorporate curved, flowing edges rather than rigid right angles in planting areas. Water features, or stones that represent water, can be used to accomplish this. To promote the flow of air, avoid crowding plants, trees, or shrubs together or placing them where they will touch the house. Selecting plants with a variety of forms and foliage is also said to increase the flow of energy.

Secret or concealed gardens are important in feng shui gardening, particularly if they are sited and planned to build on a specific aspect or direction, such as an Inner Knowledge area.

Evergreen trees and shrubs are said to embody the wood element (one of the five natural elements—wood, fire, earth, metal, and water). Healthy specimens act as guardians and attract positive energy.

Dead or sickly plants are a harmful influence, obstructing the flow of energy. Replace all dead or unhealthy plants to promote energy flow.

RIGHT: *Though its form is simple and ancient, the labyrinth still holds wonder today. Used for walking meditations, the labyrinth is also an arresting visual feature.*

LABYRINTHS AND MAZES

While we may think of labyrinths and mazes as almost interchangeable, in fact they are quite distinct, at least modern terms. A maze is a puzzle-like structure made up of walls or a tall, dense, usually evergreen hedge; filled with dead ends and twists and turns, it is designed to confuse and mystify those who walk its paths. This form of garden maze was created in Italy about six hundred years ago.

Labyrinth designs most likely evolved from spirals observed in nature. The oldest labyrinth patterns have been traced back to more than 3000 B.C.—some say as far back as 6,500 B.C.—and can be found in the cultural history of the ancient Romans, Greeks, Cretans, Syrians, Celts, Christians, and Native Americans (primarily the Hopi and Navajo of the southwestern United States and the Pima tribe of South America).

Labyrinths, unlike mazes, are unicursal, which means they have a single path that leads to the center. The current popularity of unicursal labyrinths can be traced back to early Christian tradition, when the single "true" path was viewed as a metaphor for life. This design was originally developed for installation on church floors to provide a pattern for sacred dances.

Today there are two widely copied unicursal patterns: the seven-circuit Cretan-style labyrinth, which dates to at least 2000 B.C. and is reputed to be patterned on the orbit of Mercury as seen from Earth, and the eleven-circuit Chartres-style labyrinth, a complex pattern forty-two feet (12.8m) wide that was installed at the cathedral in Chartres, France, in the year 1201. Both of these classic labyrinth patterns, as well as other variations, have been rediscovered and adapted for spiritual use by people of many religions and denominations. Others without religious affiliation recommend "walking the labyrinth" as a walking meditation, and have created their own labyrinths in parks, forests, public places, and in their own gardens.

A labyrinth can be painted on canvas, inlaid with flat rocks or stepping stones into a base of turf, pine needles, or crushed gravel, or even set into concrete. The trick to walking a labyrinth is to walk slowly, putting one foot carefully in front of the other, without straying off the path. Since the single path will eventually lead to the center, it is not necessary to focus on where the path is taking you. As in the journey of life, it is the journey itself that is important. The simple act of following the path of a labyrinth, a symbolic spiritual journey, seems to bring about an amazing sense of serenity and harmony.

157

Resources

Anderson Design
P.O. Box 4057 C
Bellingham, WA 98227
800-947-7697
Arbors, trellises, gates, and pyramids (Oriental, modern, and traditional style)

Barlow Tyrie Inc.
1263 Glen Avenue Suite 230
Moorestown, NJ 08057-1139
609-273-7878
Teak wood garden furniture in English garden style

Boston Turning Works
42 Plymouth Street
Boston, MA 02118
617-482-9085
Distinctive wood finials for gates, fenceposts, and balustrades

Brown Jordan
9860 Gidley Street
El Monte, CA 91731
(818) 443-8971
Outdoor furniture

Charleston Gardens
61 Queen Street
Charleston, SC 29401
803-723-0252
Fine garden furnishings

Florentine Craftsmen Inc.
46-24 28th Street
DepartmentGD
Long Island City, NY 11101
718-937-7632
Garden furniture, ornaments, fountains and staturary of lead, stone, and bronze

FrenchWyres
P.O. Box 131655
Tyler, TX 75713
903-597-8322
Wire garden furnishings: trellis, urns, cachepots, window boxes, arches, and plant stands

Giati Designs, Inc.
614 Santa Barbara Street
Santa Barbara, CA 93101
(805) 965-6535
Teak furniture, sun umbrellas, and exterior textiles

Hooks Lattice
7949 Silverton Avenue #903
San Diego, CA 92126
1-800-896-0978
Handcrafted wrought-iron gardenware

Kenneth Lynch & Sons
84 Danbury ROad
P.O. Box 488
WIlton, CT 06897
203-762-8363
Benches, gates, scupture and statuary, planters and urns, topiary, sundials, and weathervanes

Kinsman Company
River Road
Department351
Point Pleasant, PA 18950
800-733-4146
European plant supports, pillars, arches trellises, flowerpots, and planters

Lake Creek Garden Features Inc.
P.O. Box 118
Lake City, IA 51449
712-464-8924
Obelisks, plant stands, and gazing globes and stands

Liteform Designs
P.O. Box 3316
Portland, OR 97208
503-253-1210
Garden lighting: path, bullard, accent, step, and tree fixtures

Lloyd Flanders
3010 10th Street
P.O. Box 550
Menominee, MI 49858
(906) 863-4491
All-weather wicker furniture

New Blue Moon Studio
P.O. Box 579
Leavenworth, WA 98826
509-548-4754
Trellises, gates, arbors, and garden furniture

New England Garden Ornaments
P.O. Box 235
38 East Brookfield Road
North Brookfield, MA 01535
508-867-4474
Garden fountains and statuary, planters and urns, antique furniture, sundials, and limestone ornaments

Outdoor Lifestyle Inc.
918 N. Higland Street
Gastonia, NC 28052
(800) 294-4758
Leisure and outdoor furniture

Stone Forest
Department G
P.O. Box 2840
Sante Fe, NM 87504
505-986-8883
Hand-carved granite birdbaths, basins, fountains, lanterns, and spheres

Sycamore Creek
P.O. Box 16
Ancram, NY 12502
Handcrafted copper garden furnishings

Tanglewood Conservatories
Silver Spring, MD
Handcrafted period glass houses and atriums

Tidewater Workshop
Oceanville, NJ 08231
800-666-8433
White cedar benches, chairs, swings, and tables

Toscano
17 East Campbell Street
Department G881
Arlington Heights, IL 60005
800-525-1733
Historic garden sculptures, including seraphs and cherubs, and French tapestries

158

Valcovic Cornell Design
Box 380
Beverly, MA 01915
Trellises and arbor benches (traditional to contemporary style)

Wood Classics
Box 96G0410
Gardiner, NY 12525
914-255-5651
Garden benches, swings, chairs and tables, rockers, lounges, andumbrellas (all teak and mahogany outdoor furniture)

AUSTRALIA

Country Farm Perennials
RSD Laings Road
Nayook VIC 3821

Cox's Nursery
RMB 216 Oaks Road
Thrilmere NSW 2572

Honeysuckle Cottage Nursery
Lot 35 Bowen Mountain Road
Bowen Mountain via Grosevale NSW 2753

CANADA

Corn Hill Nursery Ltd.
RR 5
Petitcodiac NB EOA 2HO

Ferncliff Gardens
SS 1
Mission, British Columbia
V2V 5V6

McFayden Seed Co. Ltd.
Box 1800
Brandon, Manitoba
R7A 6N4

Stirling Perennials
RR 1
Morpeth, Ontario
N0P 1X0

Index

159

Photo Credits